Travels in Provence

MEREHURST PRESS
LONDON

Peillon

Travels in Provence

Marion Deschamps

MEREHURST PRESS
LONDON

For Chris and Alex

Published 1988 by Merehurst Press
5 Great James Street
London, WC1N 3DA

Copyright © Marion Deschamps 1987
All rights reserved

First published in Great Britain in 1987 by
Phoenix Publishing Associates Ltd

ISBN 1 85391 031 7

Printed in Great Britain by Hartnolls Limited, Bodmin
Cornwall

Typeset by Margaret Spooner Typesetting
Designed and produced by Snap! Books
Illustrations by Anne Forrest
Maps by Sue Lawes

Contents

St. Paul de Vence

Author's Preface

The often quoted 'France is all things to all men' is no less true, I think, for Provence. The great natural attractions found here of climate, scenery and vegetation have an irresistible appeal. While the individual traveller may settle, according to taste, for the highlife of the Riviera or the inland regions of old Provence.

Travel and gastronomy have always gone hand in hand, and having written an equal number of books on both is proof, I think, that this is particularly true for me. Eating out to me has always been one of the best kinds of entertainment. Moreover, when a particular dish appeals, the chef is always happy to discuss it, with no pretence of a secret he cannot disclose. Although I have suggested restaurants for each day, it is always worth having a look at the menus, attached by law outside every establishment, before making your final choice. There may well be occasions, too, when you are happy just to sit over a glass of white wine in a local café before taking a picnic lunch out into the country or up into the hills.

To ask 'Why go to Provence?' is like asking a mountaineer why he climbs a mountain. My own personal addiction is for that part which is evoked by Cézanne in his painting, Mistral in his poetry and Alphonse Daudet in his prose, typified in the ochres and pinks, faded by wind and sun, of its houses with their pantiled roofs; in the barren expanses of scrubland dotted with olives, pines and cypresses, where the only sounds are the cries of countless crickets. It is typified, too, in the endless games of boules beneath the plane trees on the village square.

I must have first been aware of Provence on reading Daudet's 'Lettres de Mon Moulin', so clearly and simply told that from childhood they seemed the best way to portray this land to the British reader. Often foreign travel can mean food all too frequently as easily obtainable in a hotel of the same class at home. But in France it really is very difficult to eat badly. And Provence, being so popular a holiday ground, offers restaurants to suit all purses whether you decide on a small one full of local colour or a slap-up establishment.

The old Provence has a great sense of antiquity, where traditions have survived and where every church and castle evokes her history. The land is impregnated with her Roman past, her identity surviving even where only ruins remain.

By contrast the name of the Côte d'Azur still holds a certain magic, albeit as the playground of the rich. For me the luxury yachts also have their charm, as do the well-tended gardens with their marvellous beds of cyclamen, the palms and the oleanders bordering the boulevards, the carnivals and the flower festivals.

The hill towns and perched villages have a different fascination, one can look down from their heights on to a mosaic of lavender and carnations, violets and roses according to the season.

For flowers really to typify Provence, and I have only to close my eyes as I look into a flower shop in Paris or London to imagine myself back in the south of France.

Introduction to Provence

History

Provence derives its name from the fact that it was the first Roman province beyond the Alps. And although today it consists of five *departements* (or counties) one seldom uses these except on maps and for administrative purposes. To name them, however, they are the Bouches-du-Rhône, Vaucluse, Alpes de Haute Provence, Alpes Maritimes and Var. One can almost say that Provence exists wherever there are olive trees and the mistral, that fierce wind which sweeps down the Rhône and sometimes blows for days.

Before the time of the Romans the Ligurians had already settled here, although all that remains to show for their existence are numerous ruined fortresses on the summits of hills along the coast. After the Ligurians, Provence was colonised by the Greeks. Since the time of the Romans, whose influence has remained throughout the province, Provence suffered civil strife and invasions; invasions from the Visigoths, Franks and Saracens, the mark of the last named still remaining in many a hill village. Even in the present century it suffered invasion by the Germans and Italians during the last war.

From the fourteenth century until 1860 the river Var was the frontier between France and Italy. The present *departement* of the Var is, in fact, a misnomer, since the river now runs through what is the departement of the Alpes Maritimes. Until 1860 the frontier of France ended at St. Laurent du Var on the west bank of the river.

Geography

Despite the vagaries of its history Provence has managed to keep its own special character and individuality, albeit there are really two regions, maritime and inland.

Inland Provence is highly varied, from the sheltered plain of the Rhône and the lower Durance in the west, to the mountains, hills and gorges of the east. If much of the coastal region has bowed to the demands of progress, it has still the marvellous azur of its sea, the red rocks of the Esterel, sandy coves beneath the shade of pines and cork oaks, and the calanques, small fjords whose rocky cliffs plunge almost vertically down to the sea. This coastline is flanked by a varied scenery, from sloping vineyards of the Rhône valley to hills with their perched villages, spectacular gorges and the range of the Maures, the Alpilles, and the imposing Alps of Provence. Geographically, Provence stretches between natural boundaries from the Riviera as far as Menton eastwards, and westwards as far as the marshy Carmargue. In all it is shaped like an amphitheatre rising to the rocky summits of the Massif du Ventoux and the Alpes de Haute Provence. This geographical situation ensures an excellent climate and the maximum number of hours of sunshine.

Agriculture and Industry

The three traditional crops of Provence are corn, vines and olives. The extraction of oil from the olives produces, of course, olive oil, but the final, inferior pressing is used in soap. The *savon de Marseille* is popular domestically. Marseilles, of course, is the most important port of France. Early fruit and vegetables are produced including melons from Cavaillon, peaches from Fréjus, and truffles from around Carpentras and figs from round Marseilles. In the Vaucluse the tinning of fruit and vegetables has become an important industry. Flowers and perfume also have a commercial value, while the use of its wood is also important, olive and, in particular, cork of which the production in Provence is renowned worldwide. There is fishing along the coast but the catches are insufficient to supply the region's own needs.

There are petrol refineries, extraction of ochre and bauxite, the latter mineral having taken its name from Les Baux where it was first discovered in its rocks in 1822 and which provides the basis for aluminium. Production round Les Baux ceased many years ago. It is now being produced in the region of Brignoles although here, too, the exploitation is nearly exhausted and prospecting is underway for new sites.

The Epicure's Guide

Food

Visitors to Provence will soon become familiar with such traditional snacks as the simple *ban bagnat* and the less well known *socca* delicious hot pancakes made with chick pea flour and olive oil and seasoned with black pepper. One must remember, however, that there are really two Provences; the *coastal districts* and the *haute Provence*, as sung by Giano and Marcel Pagnol, where the cookery is that of the shepherd, simple but fragrant with herbs — thyme, rosemary and basil.

Provençal lamb, in fact, is particularly famed for its flavour, nourished by the aromatic plants of the mountains. *Epaule de mouton aux olives* and *gigot en croute* are both delicious. Lamb has remained more popular than beef in mountain districts, a custom that has survived from the past when beef was seldom obtainable in the isolated villages.

In the *coastal districts* the Greek and Roman influence is evident in the spiciness of the sauces. Here fish and seafood reign supreme — culminating in the divine *bouillabaisse*, a combination of fish so rich that it is almost a meal in itself. There are, of course, almost as many varieties as there are fishing harbours, but the essential basis is a selection of very fresh fish, good olive oil and best quality saffron. Although most cooks add white wine in the cooking, purists will tell you that even this detracts from the flavour of the fish. But they will tell you, too, that it is an essential accompaniment. *Rascasse*, a tiny fish found in the rocks, is an essential of *bouillabaisse*.

Pieds paquets, made with tripe, is a speciality around Marseilles. Even more delicious, if one should happen upon them, are the *doublo de biou*, tripe simmered in vin de Cassis. To-day veal is also popular and less expensive than in other parts of France.

All kinds of sea-food have always been popular along the Mediterranean coast. Cockles and crayfish, mussels and sea-urchin, served sometimes with vinaigrette dressing, sometimes eaten raw.

In the region of the Camargue you may be served *tellines*, a delicious kind of cockle that they gather in the sands, and serve with a sharp sauce. You may also, sometimes, find eels from the Rhône on the menu, served in a variety of ways, including smoked.

Essentially Mediterranean fish are *loup de mer* (sea-perch) and *rouget* (red mullet). Rouget is delicious served cold, and loup de mer either *au fenouil* (with fennel) or *grillé aux sarments de vigne* (grilled in vine branches). *Estofic*, their way with fresh cod, may sometimes be on the menu. The word is the Niçois translation of *stockfisch*, which tradition relates was first introduced here by a Dutch sailor who gave it in exchange for a song.

Brandade is the Provençal way with salt cod, sometimes made extra good by the addition of truffles.

Although *bouillabaisse* so typifies the Mediterranean coast, their fish soup is no less popular and often appears on restaurant menus, usually accompanied by a bowl of grated cheese and *rouille*, a sauce that goes well, too, with fish.

In mountainous districts salads often replace soup in warm weather, but the salads will be those found wild, dandelions, wild chicory and salsify.

Like everywhere in France soup is popular, the most typical in Provence is *l'aigo boulido*, which is simply water boiled with a pinch of salt and plenty of crushed garlic and poured over slices of bread, previously soaked in olive oil. Although the bourgeois of Aix used, in the past, to break an egg per person into the *aigo*. Today, this habit is more widespread. Of the vegetable soups, the *pistou* has probably as many versions as does the *bouillabaisse*, the one ingredient common to all being that it should be highly flavoured with basil. In fact, it is often imagined that the word *pistou* is Provençal for basil, whereas, actually, it is derived from a kind of basil paste, made by pounding in a mortar with a *pistoun*, or pestle.

Daubes, estouffades and *broufados* are popular ways of cooking meat or poultry and vegetables, simmered very slowly in a sealed utensil called a daubière; hence the term *en daube*. Aix claims the supremacy of its own variety, called the

Croix de Malte and originally learned from the peasants of the neighbouring village of Equilles.

Gastronomes claim that olives and garlic are the predominant features of all Provençal cooking. Poets calls garlic 'that divine condiment' while a Provençal proverb declares that fish should live in the sea but cook in olive oil.

Garlic, of course, is a vegetable even if, on account of its strong flavour, it is commonly considered more as a condiment. It is at its most pungent in aioli which is, in reality, no more than a simple mayonnaise to which plenty of crushed garlic is added. It can be served with all fish dishes, soups, and is even a popular accompaniment to cold meat.

Cheeses are made chiefly from the milk of goats and ewes, depending on local resources: brousse, ventoux and banon, covered with rosemary leaves, tommes d'Arles, picodon de Valreas. Nearly every village has its own cheese, nameless but creamy and all are delicious on rye bread.

The climate of Provence provides a wonderful variety of fruit and vegetables: egg plants and fennel, courgettes and artichokes are plentiful both on the market stall and on the restaurant menu. Rather surprisingly, *tourte à la courge* (pumpkin pie) is very popular. So, too, are tiny broad beans often eaten raw with salt when they are called *croque au sel*. Vegetables are often served as an hors d'oeuvre rather than as an accompaniment to the main course. As well as broad beans, baby artichoke hearts are eaten raw, spinach is served *en bouillabaisse*, egg-plants stuffed and flowers of courgettes in fritters.

Ratatouille, a vegetable stew of Arab origin, makes an excellent accompaniment to all meats or served on it own with the addition of eggs. The origin of its name is interesting, *touiller*, in Provençal, meaning 'to stir'; *tatouille* — 'to stir a second time' and *ratatouille* evidently three times or more. Anyway the vegetables certainly need to be well stirred during their cooking.

Pezises, found in the region of Aix, are fragile, tulip shaped mushrooms that do marvels for an omelette. Truffles are plentiful around Carpentras, for although one always associates these with the Périgord, 75% of the variety known as the *truffe de Périgord* are, in fact, grown in the Vaucluse.

As starters, Provence has her share of *charcuterie* with saucisson d'Arles and andouillette de l'Ile-sur-Sorgue, jambon de montagne and pâté de grives.

Also popular is tapenade, which consists of stoned black olives, anchovy fillets and capers pounded to a paste. In Provençal *tapeno* means capers, which are, as can be tasted, an important ingredient of this dish.

Fruit is abundant, green figs and strawberries, grapes and cherries, melons, peaches and apricots, and prunes from Brignoles. Fruit, in fact, is the most usual way to end a meal and, according to the great Provençal chef Escoffier, the ideal way. But he also added that it was even better when accompanied with ice-cream and it was he who invented the exquisite *Pêche Melba* for the great Australian singer, Nellie Melba.

In Provence many observe the ancient Christmas custom whereby on Christmas Eve, after a day of fasting and Midnight Mass, the meal consists of fish and thirteen desserts. But these are sweets or produce of the local baker, for they include *calisssons d'Aix, nougat noir,* crystallised melon, and *bonbons en papillotes* (the sweets have a fizzling firework attached), *étoiles à la canelle* and *méringues aux amandes.* Other specialities for the sweet tooth include *biscotins* from Aix, *berlingots* from Carpentras, *calabrons* from Nîmes, almond-flavoured biscuits and chocolates from Tarascon, crystallised fruit from Apt, nougat from Sault and the Gâteau St. Tropez, a wonderfully light spongecake, thick with cream.

At Nyons black olives are wedged in slices of *mordade*, a bread containing crystallised fruit.

Wine

The vine has been cultivated in Provence since antiquity. Records show that it was already present when the Phoceans landed in Marseilles around 600 B.C. Later the Romans continued its cultivation, after which its production was taken up with enthusiasm by the nobility. The enthusiasm of Réné, Count of Provence, was such that he became known as *le roi-vigneron.* Then Eleanor of Provence, wife of England's Henry III, spread the reputation of these wines as had her celebrated grandmother, Eleanor of Aquitaine.

Although Provence, of course, can never be compared with Bordeaux, nevertheless, for the departement of Var alone wine represents 45 per cent of her agricultural produce, covering 51 per cent of her surface. *Carignan* and *Cinsault* are the principle grape varieties: the *Carignan* has a strong alcoholic content and lightly metallic taste, the *Cinsault* is more mellow with a distinctive bouquet.

Best known are the very popular *Côtes de Provence*, with the advantage of their great versatility, accompanying, as they do, almost any meal. For many holiday-makers they have come to symbolise holidays in the sun. Their production is the most prolific of all Provençal wines, although their quality varies considerably, depending on whether they are château-bottled or blended from different vineyards. Sometimes the distinctive character of individual growths can be lost in the blending. Many of these vineyards of Provence are small, with the result that more than half the production goes to the co-operatives. In recent years, however, growers have concentrated on improving their quality rather than quantity.

The prodigious wines of *Cassis* were already celebrated in the eleventh century — red, rosé and, above all, white of which the poet Mistral declared that they had an aroma of rosemary, heather and myrtle. They make a good accompaniment to fish and seafood.

The slopes of the Rhône valley produce the *Côteau d'Aix*, but the multiplicity of grape varieties is such that the quality of their wines, mostly red and rosé, varies considerably.

Of considerable repute, too, are the wines of *Bandol*. There are white and rosé, but best known is the red, an excellent accompaniment to meat and game, and a wine which ages well. The vineyards cover quite a large area in the region of Bandol.

A wine that has only relatively recently been judged a V.D.Q.S. is that produced in the region of *Brignoles*.

A number of vineyards are open to visitors, the wine can be tasted and, of course, bought. But often an appointment has to be made in advance since most small growers are not organised to receive visitors on a large scale but always welcome a small party. In the listing below I have, however, tried as far as possible to give those where no appointment is necessary.

Caves Co-operatives de Beaumes-de-Venise Vaucluse. In the comfortable tasting rooms here you will be offered the delicately flavoured Muscats, as well as Rasteau, another dessert wine, and Gigondas, a rich red table wine, both of which are produced in neighbouring communes.

Château St. Jean-de l'Hôpital Gignac-la-Nerthe, 13700 Marignane, tel. 4288 5515. These vineyards produce wines of the Côteaux d'Aix. Tastings by appointment.

Mas de la Dame Les Baux-de-Provence. The red wine of this vineyard was lauded by Van Gogh. It also produces a delicious rosé. Tastings daily between 8 a.m and 7 p.m.

Château de Calissane 13680 Lançon-de-Provence, tel. 9042 6303 (close to Salon-de-Provence). This vineyard produces an excellent red Côteau-d'Aix. Tastings by appointment.

Domaine de la Vallonge 13810 Eygalières, tel. 9095 9170. This vineyard produces delicious and unusual wines. Tastings by appointment.

Terres Blanches 13210 St. Rémy-de-Provence. Termed the Côteaux de Baux-de-Provence, the wines of this vineyard have the aroma of the Alpilles where they are situated. Tastings every day except Sundays from 8 a.m.-12.00 p.m. and 2-6 p.m.

Château Grand Seuil Puyricard, 13540 Aix-en-Provence. The castle to which this vineyard belongs is a small gem of Provençal architecture, its light rosé wine is delicious. Tastings every day from 9 a.m.-12.00 p.m. and 2-6.30 p.m.

Château Baron Georges 13114 Puyloubier, tel. 9459 4868. This domaine, protected from the mistral by the mountain of Sainte-Victoire, produces a light, perfumed rosé de Provence. Tastings by appointment.

Domaine de Duffends 83470 St. Maximin-la-Ste.-Beaume. This small vineyard produces a delicious rosé Côte Varois, one of the newly classed VDQS. Tastings every day except Sundays from 9 a.m.-7 p.m.

Domaine de Barbaroux, Brignoles. This vineyard produces a very high quality red Côte Varois. Tastings every day from 8 a.m.-12.00 p.m. and 2-6 p.m.

Close Boudard Route de la Ciotat, Cassis. This small, family-run vineyard produces a delicious white wine of Cassis. Tastings every day from 8 a.m.-12.00 p.m. and 1-6 p.m.

Domaine de la Noblesse 83740 La Cadière d'Azur (reached by turning off at Les Lecques on to the D66 for 5 miles). Ancient property of a certain Sire Noble, the domaine has kept up the same high standard of Bandol wine. Tastings every day from 8 a.m.-12.00 p.m. and 2-6 p.m.

Domaine de la Jeannette, 83400 Hyères. A fine bastide is surrounded by the vineyards which produce an excellent rosé of Provence. Tastings every day except Sundays from 8 a.m.-12.00 p.m. and 2-6 p.m.

Domaine de l'Ile Ferme de Breganconnet, Ile de Porquerolles, tel. 9458 3160. Two vineyards here produce a red wine as well as their celebrated rosé which maintains the tradition of the island. Tastings by appointment.

Domaine de la Malherbe, 83230 Bormes-les-Mimosas. These vineyards alongside the Presidential Fort of Bregançon are a delight to the eye as are its wines to taste. Tastings every day from 9 a.m.-12 p.m. and 2-6 p.m.

Domaine de la Croix 83420 La Croix-Valmer, tel. 9879 6002. This is one of the oldest vineyards of Provence, looking down over the bay of St. Tropez and produces a light red wine. Tastings every day from 8 a.m.-12 p.m. and 2-6 p.m.

Domaine des Launes La Garde-Freinet. Close to La Croix-Valmer, this vineyard produces a light red wine. Tastings every day from 8 a.m.-12 p.m. and 2 p.m.-6 p.m.

Vignerons Presqu'Ile Saint-Tropez This society represents a dozen vineyards giving an original variety for the tastings from Mondays to Fridays from 8 a.m.-12 p.m. and 2-7.30 p.m.

Château Saint-Maur Route de Collobrières, 83310 Cogolin, tel. 9456 0925. This vineyard produces a blanc de blancs considered one of the best white wines of Provence. Tastings by appointment.

Château de Bellet St. Romaine-de-Bellet, 06200 Nice, tel. 9337 8157. These tiny vineyards situated above Nice produce a white wine that is almost unique. Tastings by appointment.

Château de Cremat 442, Chemin de Cremat, 06200 Nice, tel. 9337 8030. Also situated on the heights above Nice, this vineyard produces a delicious red wine, high in alcohol content but light to taste. Tastings by appointment.

THE CLASSES OF WINE

1. Appellations d'Origine Contrôlées — A.O.C. Guaranteed not only of origin but of a certain standard, administered by the Central 'Institut National des Appellations d'Origine' in Paris.
2. V.D.Q.S. — Vin Délimité de Qualité Supérieure. Good wines of chiefly local interest.
3. Vins de Pays — introduced in 1973 to give recognition to the more modest wine producer previously disregarded, but whose output is well worth investigation.
4. Co-operatives — A central wine-making factory owned by the farmers (with bank backing) where they produce their wines efficiently and economically.

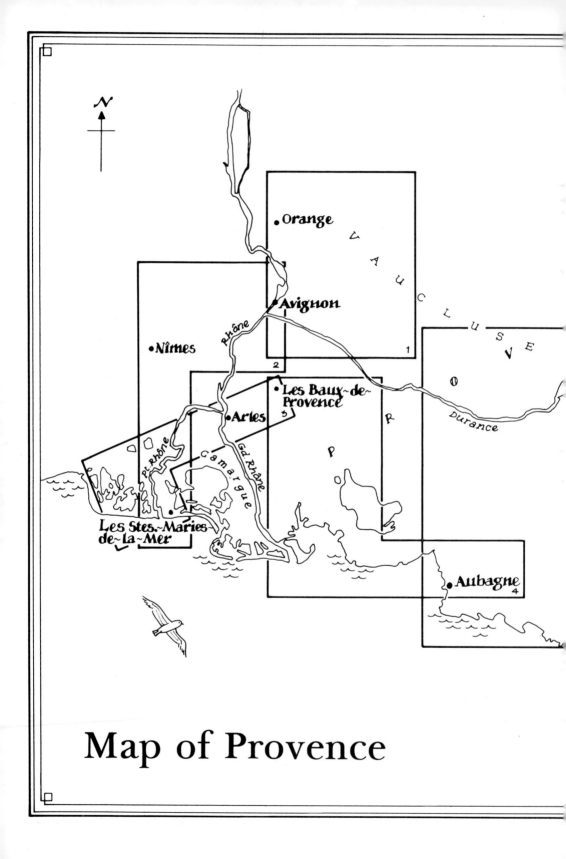

Map of Provence

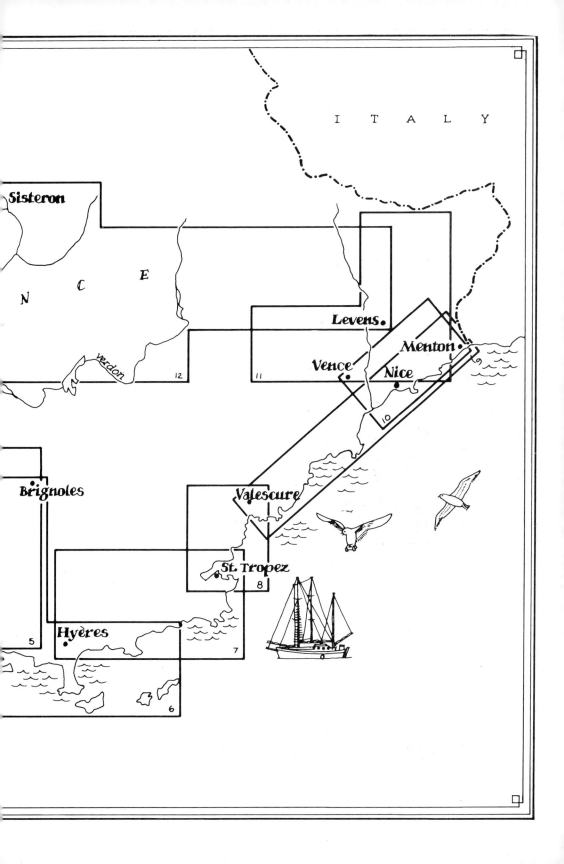

Handy Tips

HOW TO GET THERE FROM THE UK
By Air Main airports at Marseilles and Nice can be used to connect with either local air or rail services. It is advisable to reserve a hire car at your destination in high season.

By Rail The swiftest service is from Victoria Station to Marseilles via Paris which can be done with or without your car.

By Car It is advisable to allow 24 hours driving time. The autoroutes obviously offer the most direct route — but this can add £30-£50 on to your travelling costs.

WHEN TO GO
Any time from Easter to the end of September. In a good Autumn, warm sunny weather will last to the end of October.

Try to avoid travelling on or just before or after a bank holiday (see below). The worst time for traffic is the first weekend in August, when nearly every French family is on the move. Along the coast the traffic can be very difficult indeed throughout June to September.

HOTELS
It is advisable to book hotels in advance especially between July and September.

CAMPING AND CARAVANNING
There are some wonderful sites throughout Provence. Buy the green Michelin Camping and Caravanning guide for addresses. Unlike dreary England even the smallest of sites has electricity. N.B. Don't forget your Caravan Club of Great Britain registration carnet.

DRIVING
Driving on the right is usually no problem, the danger only comes when returning to the road from a car park, a petrol station and of course at roundabouts. Until recently priority was always given to those approaching from the right. This custom is fast changing and roundabouts can therefore be treated in the English style, but beware drivers turning from small roads in towns and country lanes. Traffic police can be tough even on foreign motorists who are caught speeding, overshooting a red light or failing to wear seat belts, so take care. Seat belts are obligatory everywhere in France outside town limits.

ROAD NUMBERS
The French government, which used to be responsible for numbering all the roads in

France, has started to hand over this responsibility to the individual départements. In their wisdom the individual départements have in some cases decided to renumber the roads and as you can imagine this process is not only slow but confusing. I have tried to be as correct as possible with the road numbers, but you may unfortunately find some discrepancies. For example you could come across a road marked as the N137 when it is really the D937.

SPEED LIMITS

Autoroutes	130 kmph (80 mph)	Other Roads	90 kmph (56 mph)
Dual Carriageways	110 kmph (68 mph)	Built-up areas	60 kmph (37 mph),
		or as directed by signs	

Autoroutes nearly all have periodic tolls (péages) and can be expensive on long journeys.

THE METRIC SYSTEM

Kilometres — for road distances 8 km equals 5 miles thus:

Km:miles	Km:miles	Km:miles	Km:miles
3:2	8:5	40:25	90:56
4:2½	9:5½	50:31	100:62
5:3	10:6	60:37	125:78
6:3½	20:12	70:44	150:94
7:4	30:18	80:50	200:125

BANK HOLIDAYS

New Year's Day	1st January	Whit Monday	2nd Monday after Ascension
Easter Monday	Variable		
Labour Day	1st May	Bastille Day	14th July
V.E. Day	8th May	Assumption	15th August
Ascension Day	6th Thursday after Easter	All Saints (Toussaint)	1st November
		Armistice Day	11th November
		Christmas Day	25th December

BANKS

Banks are shut on Saturdays and Sundays, except in towns with a Saturday market, when they open on Saturday and shut on Monday. Banks also close at midday on the eve of bank holidays. Banking hours are normally 8 a.m.–12 noon and 2–4.30 p.m. When changing cheques or travellers cheques remember your passport and Eurocheque encashment card or other internationally recognised cheque card.

SHOP OPENING TIMES

These vary according to a) season b) type of shop c) size of town. In most places shops are open on Saturday, but may be shut on Monday. Food shops (baker, butcher, general store) tend to shut later than others, sometimes as late as 7 p.m., some open on Sundays and bank holiday mornings. Generally all shops close for 2–3 hours at lunchtime from midday.

RAILWAYS

S.N.C.F. — Société Nationale de Chemin de Fer. The trains are generally very clean, comfortable and punctual. It is best to buy tickets in advance from mainline stations or travel agents. Seats can be reserved on main lines. Hire cars can be booked in advance in most large towns. Bicycles can be hired at stations. Men over 65 and women over 60, on production of their passport, can obtain a 'carte vermeil' entitling them to a 50% reduction on non-rush hour trains.

Note: Many stations have automatic punch ticket machines (red machine) on the platform, this dates your ticket. If you do not get your ticket punched by one of these machines you can be charged again, plus a fine of 20%, so be careful.

MONUMENTS AND MUSEUMS

Opening times and prices of admission have not been included in this book, as they are subject to change. All places mentioned are open to the public and will charge a few francs admission. Normally they will be open from Easter to the end of October, from 9.30–12.00 a.m. and from 3–5 p.m.

Note: Guided tours will cease admission half an hour before closing. Check with the local tourist office for details.

KEY TO ITINERARY

Ratings are for prices/room/night.

★★	Reasonable	★★★★	Expensive
★★★	Average	★★★★★	Very expensive

Names of the hotels and restaurants which are the first choice of the author are printed in **bold** and are distinguished by the following symbols:

Lunch   Dinner

The itinerary provides a basic route for each day and, for those with time available, offers suggestions for additional trips marked in the text as Detours.

TEXT MAPS

For simplicity, the maps in the Itinerary section follow the text by reading from left to right regardless of their actual north/south orientation. The map on page 18 provides a complete picture of the 12 days' routes.

Itinerary

DAY 1

Orange to Villeneuve-lès-Avignon: approx 100 miles.

Reaching Orange on the A7 there is much of interest in this ancient Roman city, including the ancient theatre erected about the year 1 B.C., and the cathedral. A detour can be made to Châteauneuf-du-Pape. Otherwise the D975 should be taken to Vaison-la-Romaine, one of the most beautiful and interesting towns of Provence, where excavations continue to this day. Sixteen miles separate Séguret from Carpentras, while mountain lovers can make a detour round the Mont Ventoux.

Then continue down through the enchanting little town of l'Isle-sur-la-Sorgue to Fontaine-de-Vaucluse, forever associated with the great Italian poet, Petrarch, the hill-top village of Gordes and the great abbey of Sénanque.

Turning eastwards, fifteen miles brings us to Villeneuve-lès-Avignon, taking the circular road around Avignon. Villeneuve is inseparable from Avignon and at least a visit should be made to the Fort St. André.

Travels in Provence

Travellers striking south down the A7 will notice, soon after Donzère, the first olive trees and already a new warmth in the air which spells the Midi. One enters Provence at the admirable Arc de Triomph of Orange.

Orange

This triumphal arch, built around the year 20 A.D., is one of the most handsome and best preserved in the Roman world. It consists of three vaulted arches, the central one being the highest. Eight Corinthian columns support the massive structure, decorated with figures of Roman legionaires.

Orange, the ancient Arausio, was an important Roman colony and has preserved a number of fine monuments. The theatre was built at a slightly earlier period than the Archway, in the first century B.C. Its impressive frontage, 345 ft. long and 125 ft. high, is magnificent in its solidity and the rigorous simplicity of its lines. Louis XIV was so proud of this façade that he called it 'the finest wall in my kingdom'. Holding over seven thousand spectators, its acoustics are excellent. From mid-July to mid-August there are performances of tragedies, operas, ballets and symphony concerts. The ancient cathedral of Nôtre-Dame is Romanesque, restored between the sixteenth and seventeenth centuries after being badly damaged during the Wars of Religion.

As was the case in many of these city states, Orange changed hands time and again down the centuries, and was officially annexed to the French Crown by the treaty of Utrecht in 1713. Its name, however, it owes to the Dutch dynasty who created a republic there in the Middle Ages. Today it is a little town of some 27,000 inhabitants, with narrow streets and squares shaded by plane trees, where a game of *boules*, so typical of Provence, is of more importance than the ochre monuments that bear witness to her prodigious past.

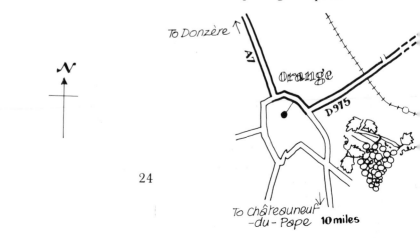

Detour

Those drawn by the name of one of the most famous wines of France may like to continue down the A7, and take the D92 to Châteauneuf-du-Pape (9 miles), whose vineyards were created by the Popes to whom the land belonged. The Musée du Père Anselm is one of viticulture, and of considerable interest showing, as it does, the presses and other medieval equipment pertaining to the vine. There is also a cellar where the wines can be tasted. Not only is the town celebrated for its vineyards, but from the imposing ruins of its castle, built by the Popes of Avignon, one has a magnificent view down over the valley of the Rhône.

For an excellent meal in a domaine of vineyards, a mile from the centre is the 3 star Hostellerie Château des Fines Roches where specialities include a *salade de truffes fraiches* (when in season) and *filet de rouget au romarin*.

Vaison-la-Romaine

Those not choosing to visit Châteauneuf should turn eastwards on the D975 to that which is certainly one of the most beautiful and interesting small towns

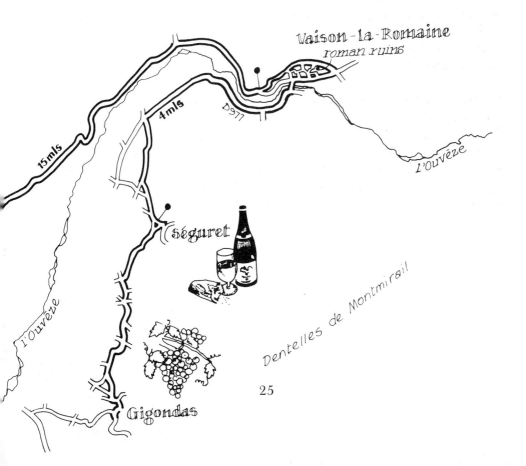

25

of Provence: Vaison-la-Romaine. Really two towns, the Gallo-Roman one is built on the banks of the river Ouvèze. Archeological excavations continue to the present day, for this ancient city, when occupied by the Romans, was one of the most prosperous in the region until devastated by barbarian invasions. Excavations have revealed, as in all these Roman cities, columns and a forum, baths and patrician dwellings, and a theatre which is a reproduction, on a smaller scale, of that of Orange.

The earliest construction of the ancient cathedral of Nôtre-Dame began in the Merovingian epoch, was destroyed by invasions and reconstructed between the eleventh and thirteenth centuries. The high altar, a simple table in marble resting on four columns, is impressive, as is also the eleventh-century cloister.

The chapel of St. Quenin used to be the subject of considerable controversy among archeologists, but it is now considered to date from the twelfth century. Across the river is a Roman bridge, arched like a rainbow. Apart from the parapet which was reinforced in the nineteenth century it has stood unchanged for two thousand years. With the troubles and unrest of the Middle Ages, the Counts of Toulouse built their medieval town on the slopes of a hill across the river, protected by ramparts and a great fortress. The narrow streets and ancient houses of this Haute Ville and the Place du Vieux Marché have kept all their medieval character. In the eighteenth century most of the population crossed the river again and re-built what is now the modern town of Vaison.

For those who feel that this would be a good time for a lunch break, there is an excellent restaurant four miles south, leaving Vaison on the D977, at Séguret, **La Table du Comtat**, where fish is a speciality. The little village of Séguret nestles beneath a hill, with an attractive fifteenth-century fountain, a fourteen-century belfry and a twelfth-century church. Its narrow streets lined by old houses, and the ruins of its feudal castle add to the charm. Séguret looks across to the sweep of the Dentelles de Montmirail, the foothills of the great mountain range of the Ventoux. Wooded with pines and oaks, the craggy ridges are an unusual formation.

Nôtre-Dame d'Aubune

Continuing south one passes through Gigondas, cultivating its vineyards, and over the Col du Cayron to Nôtre-Dame d'Aubune which takes its name from the little Roman chapel whose elegant square tower is remarkably decorated.

Beaumes-de-Venise

The adjoining village of Beaumes-de-Venise is celebrated for its vineyards. Muscat de Beaumes is mentioned by Pliny in his *Natural History*, the Provençal poet Mistral sings of it and Gounod in an opera, while in la Cave de Beaumes, as well as the famous Muscat, you can taste Côtes de Rhône and other wines. The meaning of *beaumes* is grottoes, and the village is, in fact, built into the cliffs which are riddled with grottoes. Continue south to Carpentras.

Detour

From Beaumes, mountain lovers can continue on by Malaucène, whose fourteenth-century church was built by Pope Clement V during the period that he spent here, to the summit of Mont Ventoux. It takes about an hour, but is one of the most splendid drives in Provence.

At 1909 meters, Mont Ventoux does not compare with the giants of the Alps, but its situation, with no nearby rivals, gives it an unequalled majesty with an equally unrivalled panorama across to the range of the Vercors, the Cevennes and the Montagne Ste.-Victoire, and even as far as Marseilles and the valley of the Rhône. Return to Malaucène and follow the D938 to Carpentras.

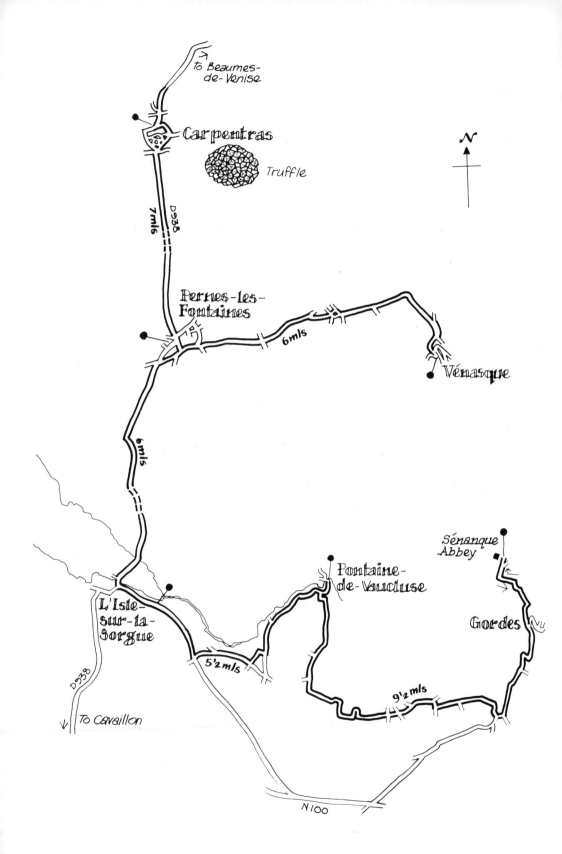

Carpentras

Carpentras is typically Provençal, the busy streets hum with activity and the markets always seem particularly animated. In times past it was the capital of the Comtat Venaissin, a Papal fief governed by a rector nominated by the Pope. All that remains of the fourteenth-century ramparts, constructed by the Popes to protect their capital, is the imposing Porte d'Orange.

There is also a small and quite well-preserved Gallo-Roman triumphal arch behind the seventeenth-century Palais de Justice where the Pope resided and which can be visited on Saturdays and Sundays. It contains some fine seventeenth-century paintings and beautiful woodwork.

The ancient cathedral was constructed at the beginning of the fifteenth century on the initiative of Pope Benoit XII. On the south side is a doorway in flamboyant style known as the Porte Juive, its name deriving from the fact that converted Jews used to enter by this door to be baptised. Benoit XII left his mark very visibly here, for at the time of the Great Schism, after being beseiged for five years in his palace at Avignon, he escaped to Carpentras on a night in March, 1403.

Other monuments of interest include the eighteenth-century Town Hall which has a magnificent wrought-iron staircase, a pharmacy whose cupboards are painted with landscapes, and comic figurines caricaturing the pharmaceutical profession, while the interior contains a fine collection of earthenware pots. There is also a chapel decorated with paintings by Mignard and Parrocel.

But perhaps the town's most original monument is the early eighteenth-century synagogue, the oldest in France. It can be visited from Mondays to Fridays and is full of interest, with galleries, panelling and wrought-iron work, as well as an oven for baking the unleavened bread and baths for purification.

Pernes-les-Fontaines

A few miles south, Pernes-les-Fontaines was capital of the Comtat Venaissin from the tenth century until 1320 when it was replaced by Carpentras. To enter it one passes beneath sixteenth-century gateways, surmounted by round machicolated towers. The Romanesque church of Nôtre-Dame-de-Nazareth was built over a crypt which, according to legend, was an oratory to St. Martha. The Tour Ferrande, a square, crenellated tower, is open to visitors by applying to the Office of Tourism or to the Mairie. It is well worth climbing the narrow staircase to the third floor which is decorated with very curious frescoes dating back to the thirteenth century when the tower was built.

Also worth noting in this attractive little town are the old fortified gateway of Nôtre-Dame with the nearby sixteenth-century bridge and the little chapel of the same period. Pernes owes its name to its thirty-two fountains of which the eighteenth-century Fontaine du Cormoran is the most impressive.

Detour

Six miles to its east, Vénasque is of special interest for its beautiful little Merovingian baptistry, one of the very rare early Christian monuments still standing. In its centre one sees the hollow for the baptismal font.

L'Isle-sur-la-Sorgue

Continue south again to l'Isle-sur-la-Sorgue, criss-crossed by branches of the river Sorgue, with avenues lined by plane trees, making it a delightful little town in which to idle. The very beautiful church is richly decorated with Italian style panelling, sculpture and paintings which are all, in fact, the work of local artists. Six old watermills, similar to those which, in the past, used to work the silk factories and the oil mills, are situated one close to the Place Gambetta, another in the Place Emile Char, two in the Boulevard Victor Hugo and two in the Rue Jean Theophile.

Fontaine-de-Vaucluse

A few miles to the east is Fontaine-de-Vaucluse, forever associated with the great Italian poet, Petrarch. There is always a touch of magic about place names which evoke the great artists and poets of the world, and I feared, as I entered this little village, that commercialism might have ruined this almost sacred spot. However, once past the pottery and postcard stalls, a path leads up to the celebrated fountain which is, in fact, a torrent that crashes down through the gorge. There are few signs of the fountain which used to gush out of the bare rock, but it remains an impressive setting.

It was here that Petrarch used to come to meditate, here that he mourned Laura, his love for whom he celebrated with the sonnets known as the *Canzonei*, which are usually divided into two collections: those written 'in vita de Madonna Laura' — during her lifetime, and those 'in morte Madonna Laura' — after her death, for she died of the plague. The story of Petrarch and Laura is, of course, one of the great love stories of all time. It was in the fourteenth century that, for the first time, he saw the beautiful Laura in a church in Avignon and fell passionately in love. But Laura was married — and virtuous — so Petrarch expressed his love as a symbol of pure intellectual beauty, of a spiritual, unobtainable paradise. We have no mention of the faintest encouragement accorded to him, and ten years after the first meeting, still only thirty-three, he retired to Vaucluse where he remained for sixteen years.

The house where he lived is now the Petrarch museum.

Gordes

Nearby Gordes is impressive in quite a different way, an extraordinary old village whose houses are built into the hillside, climbing up to the rocky promontory which is dominated by her church and her castle. The Renaissance castle was built on the site of an ancient fortress. On the first floor a monumental fireplace is splendidly decorated, while five rooms are given over to the work of the painter Vasarely.

Sénanque

It is worth continuing six miles further to the great Cistercian abbey of Sénanque, situated in a deep valley, one of the best-preserved of all the Cistercian abbeys of France, founded by St. Bernard himself in 1148. A visit is rewarding indeed, for it is one of the few such abbeys where all the monastery remains as it was in the twelfth century, including the kitchens and the huge dormitory with cross-cradled vaulting and tiny windows. One can admire, too, the splendid Romanesque church, also founded in the twelfth century, with a beautiful cloister and chapter house.

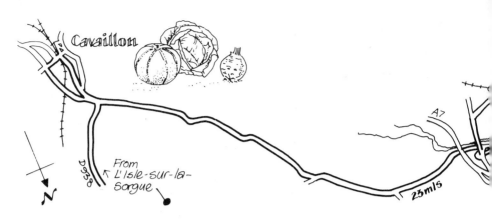

Cavaillon

After exploring this enchanting corner of the Vaucluse, one must turn back to l'Isle-sur-la-Sorgue to continue south for five miles to Cavaillon, which is famed, above all, as a market for early vegetables although it has its monuments too; a Gallo-Roman triumphal arch, a Romanesque cathedral with an attractive cloister, an eighteenth-century synagogue and an ancient Hotel-Dieu which now houses an archeological museum.

Châteaurenard

One turns north-west again to continue for fifteen miles, passing through Châteaurenard, also very important for its early vegetables and with only two towers standing of its once feudal castle, to one of the greatest cities of France, which is Avignon.

Villeneuve-lès-Avignon

Taking the loop road round Avignon brings us to Villeneuve-lès-Avignon, on the right bank of the Rhône. Villeneuve is inseparable from Avignon for it was here that the Cardinals, not finding dwellings to their liking in the Papal state, migrated across the river to build themselves magnificent mansions that are known as the Livrées. The prosperity continued after the departure of the Cardinals, and in the seventeenth and eighteenth centuries other fine mansions were built and the convents flourished until the Revolution.

The Tour Philippe le Bel was constructed by the king at the end of the Pont St.

32

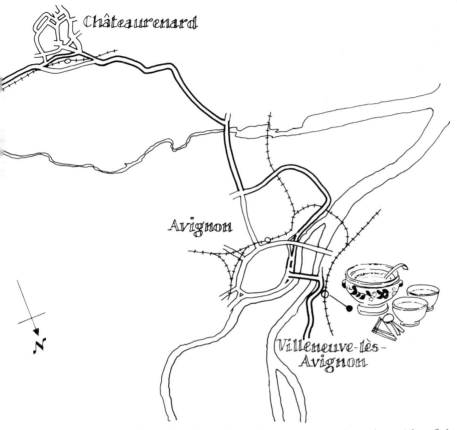

Benezet to defend his kingdom from Provence on the other side of the river. From the terrace, reached by a flight of a hundred and seventy-three steps, one has a splendid view from the realm of the kings to the realm of the popes. The Collegiate church of Nôtre-Dame, founded in 1333, has some valuable paintings and a fine altar, but its chief pride is in the vestry, the marvellous ivory statue of the Virgin which is considered a masterpiece of French sculpture. The most prestigious religious building, however, is the Chartreuse du Val de Benediction, founded by Pope Innocent VI in the fourteenth century, and the most important monument in France of this order.

After passing through the impressive entrance, one visits the church, with its side chapels and the tomb of Pope Innocent in white marble. The Petit Cloître leads into the Cour des Sacrisans which has a well and a fine staircase. The so called Cloître de Cimitière is the largest of the cloisters and surrounded by the monks' cells, while the Cloister of St. Jean has a monumental fountain, wells and a fine ancient vessel.

33

Leaving the Chartreuse by the east door one reaches the Fort St. André which dominates Villeneuve-lès-Avignon. It stands on the summit of the Mont Andaon, now more usually known as the hill of St. André. Built between 1360 and 1364 by King Jean le Bon, it is one of the best-preserved medieval military structures in existence. Once entered by a magnificent gateway, surmounted by twin towers, the precincts consist of the Benedictine abbey, the Roman chapel of Nôtre-Dame de Belvezet and sections of the walls of what used to be the borough of St. André. The terrace, eighty-five steps up and built over the twin towers, commands a wide view over Avignon and the Palace of the Popes, and across to Mont Ventoux, the Rhône and the Alpilles.

Dinner and overnight at the **Hostellerie le Prieuré**, Villeneuve-lès-Avignon.

ORANGE: USEFUL INFORMATION

Tourist Office:	Place Frères Mounet
	Tel: (90) 34 70 88
Population:	27502
Altitude:	46 metres
Facilities:	Swimming pools (outdoor and indoor), hotels

La Table du Comtat
Séguret
Tel: (90) 46 91 49

This pleasant restaurant — which has 8 rooms if you are looking for overnight accommodation — has a coveted Michelin star. The *Escalope de bar à la crème de favouilles* is delicious. Another original choice would be the *Pot au feu de pigeon*. A good accompaniment would be a Vin de Séguret which the region produces. The restaurant is closed on Wednesdays except during July and August.

Credit cards: American Express, Diner's Club, Eurocard, Visa

Hostellerie le Prieuré
Place du Chapitre
Villeneuve-lès-Avignon
Tel: (90) 25 18 20

This very comfortable family-run hotel is housed in a modernised ancient priory, set in a delightful park. Meals can be served in the garden. All rooms have air-conditioning, private bathroom and a television.

Closed:	9th November to 15th March
Rooms:	22
Facilities:	Bar, restaurant, swimming pool, tennis courts, car park.
Credit cards:	American Express, Diner's Club, Eurocard, Visa
Food:	With a Michelin star to recommend it try *Piccate de lotte au pistou* and *Corolle d'agneau rôti*.
Wine:	*Tavel*
Rating:	★★★★

LA MAGNANERAIE
37 Rue Camp-de-Bataille
Villeneuve-les-Avignon
Tel: (90) 25 11 11

This hotel is pleasant, comfortable and very good value.

VILLENEUVE-LES-AVIGNON: USEFUL INFORMATION

Tourist Office:	1 Place Ch.-David
	Tel: (90) 25 61 33
Population:	9535
Altitude:	24 metres
Facilities:	4 star camping site, Pont St Benezet Hotels, Avignon — 2 miles

Avignon — Saint Benezet Bridge

DAY 2

Villeneuve-lès-Avignon to Les Saintes-Maries-de-la-Mer: approx 61 miles.

Fourteen miles separates Villeneuve-lès-Avignon from the Pont du Gard, one of the great marvels of antiquity. However, this may be difficult to fit in since at least a morning should be devoted to Avignon with the marvellous Papal Palace.

Leaving Avignon on the N570, both Tarascon and Beaucaire would be worth a halt if time permitted. But Nîmes, considered the Rome of France, is not to be rushed, with its splendid Maison Carée, the amphitheatre and other Roman monuments.

Thirty-three miles south brings us to Les Saintes-Maries-de-la-Mer.

Travels in Provence

Breakfast at Villeneuve-lès-Avignon.

Depending upon the time available you may wish to cross the river immediately to explore Avignon instead of taking the following excursion.

Detour

Fourteen miles separate Villeneuve-lès-Avignon from the Pont du Gard, yet to make the journey is almost a must for this great aquaduct is one of the marvels of antiquity, considered the most impressive monument in Roman Gaul. The Romans attached great importance to the purity of the water for their cities, and the aquaduct supplied that of Nîmes with water from its source close to Uzès. It was constructed around the year 19 B.C. on the orders of Agrippa, so has therefore remained intact for over two thousand years. It consists of three superimposed rows of arches, the third of which carries the water. Although purely utilitarian, by the harmony of its design it ranks as a masterpiece of architecture. The variety of paths enable one to look at it from different angles. Astride the valley of the Gardon, the old ochre stones of the bridge harmonise perfectly with the surrounding rocks and the brown earth beneath.

Another nine miles brings us to the north-western limit of Provence with Uzès. It is also at the limit of a limestone plateau dominating the Alzon valley. The House of Uzès dates back to the time of Charlemagne and in the sixteenth century Charles IX made the lord of Uzès a duke. During the Wars of Religion reform was preached in the region, resulting in years of civil strife. The many interesting monuments here include the Duchy, which was the home of the noble Uzès family. A massive medieval tower dominates the Renaissance wing and the Grand Salon displays furniture and costumes of the epoch. There is also a Gothic chapel. The cathedral, which suffered considerably during the Wars of Religion, was rebuilt in the nineteenth century. All that remains of the ancient Romanesque monument is the twelfth-century tower consisting of six circular floors, a type of belfry that is unique in France.

The town has fine old mansions, ancient gateways and changing views of the three towers which dominate the city; those of the king, Bishop and Duke.

Avignon

Avignon is, of course, above all the city of the Popes, all her history seems to date from that period, a marvellous treasurehouse of the past.

Until the beginning of the fourteenth century Avignon was of no greater importance than any other Provençal town. But in 1309 an event took place which was to bring her hitherto unimagined glory, Philippe le Bel influenced the election of a French Prelate to the Holy See. To escape the constant intrigues of Rome he induced the new Pope to settle in Avignon, a town belonging to the Count of Provence — a faithful upholder of the Church. From 1305 until 1377 it was the residence of seven occupants of St. Peter's as well as of some anti-popes.

One of the most ardent supporters of the movement for the return of the Holy See to Rome was the poet Petrarch, and in 1377 Gregory XI returned to Rome and for over forty years the church was rent by what was called the Great Schism, with two rival popes, one in Rome, the other in Avignon. On approaching Avignon one must look at it from the suspension bridge across the Rhône to appreciate how the massive Palace of the Popes dominates the whole city, then drive round the medieval fortifications, still intact, crenellated and dotted with towers and gateways.

The palace is really more impressive than beautiful, being both fortress, church and residence, one of the most vast feudal castles in the world. The

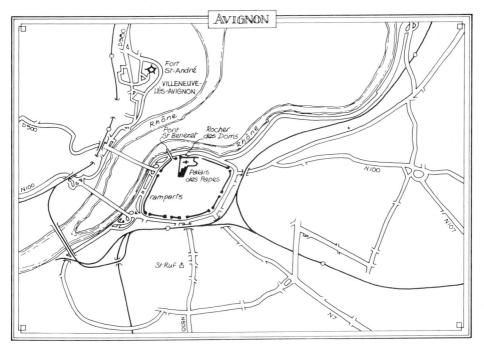

Popes needed a major military stronghold and, indeed, the French Holy See, secure within its ramparts, was to have nothing to fear. As their religion required, it was built for eternity. In style it is an extraordinary example of Gothic civil, military and religious architecture. The high walls, flanked by eight towers, enclose chapels and palaces. That of Benoit XII, or Palais Vieux, reflects the austere temperament of this once Cistercian monk, simple and unadorned. It is separated by an immense courtyard from the Palace of Clement VI or Palais Neuf which, in contrast, reflects the taste for ostentation and elegance of that great Prince of the Church.

One is struck by its emptiness, and an attempt should be made to imagine the tremendous activity of the times, when it was alive with the comings and goings of cardinals and princes, pilgrims crowding in for benediction, servants hurrying to and fro, barristers pleading. Of the chapels, that of Clementine is the most important, built over the great Audience Hall which is high and huge as a church. Two chapels superimposed one above the other in the Tower of Saint Jean are decorated with beautiful frescoes by Matteo Giovanetti, as are also Tour des Anges, the Chambres du Cerf, the Tour de la Garde-Robe. The Pope's bedchamber also has admirable secular paintings. The Great Hall is a splendid example of medieval military architecture.

The richness of this fabulous Palace within the framework of the Holy Roman Empire was made possible by the prosperity of the ruling Popes who levied heavy taxes. The Palace was badly damaged during the Revolution and during the nineteenth century it was even used as an army barracks. Restoration was undertaken at the beginning of the present century and proved long and costly. Although one cannot fail to be impressed by the Palace, it is wise not to spend too long over the visit, for there is much else to see in Avignon. The Palace overlooks an immense square surrounded by the fifteenth-century Petit Palais which was an ancient episcopal residence, and houses a remarkable collection of paintings, primitifs, French and Italian; and the Hotel des Monnaies which has a particularly beautiful façade. Also close to the Palace is the cathedral of Nôtre-Dame-des-Doms, in very pure twelfth-century Romanesque style although it has been frequently restored. The very curious mausoleum of Pope John XII is considered a masterpiece, built into the rock. This rock, part of the Rocher des Doms, is worth climbing to see the delightful gardens that have been laid out here.

The cathedral is one of the city's most ancient religious monuments, the other is the abbey church of St. Ruf. Other churches of different epochs include St.

Agricol, rich in works of art including a beautiful Renaissance reredos; St. Pierre, with beautiful fourteenth-century sculpture and woodwork; the Eglise des Carmes with her cloister and the Eglise St. Didier, remarkable for its simplicity, and the Chapel of the Penitents, now being restored, a charming small example of the religious art of the eighteenth century. The ardour to build new churches continued over the centuries, thus Rabelais was not unjustified in calling Avignon 'the ringing city' so intense was the ringing of bells. A great square tower in the Place St. Jean-le-Vieux is all that remains of the Order of St. John of Jerusalem.

One of the great art cities of France, Avignon has a wealth of museums and art galleries, including the Musée Lapidaire housed in the ancient chapel of the Jesuit college, devoted principally to furniture and porcelain; the Musée Calvet, housed in the ancient Hotel de Villeneuve, the most beautiful eighteenth-century architectural realisation in the city. It has a very fine collection of paintings including David and Gericault, Corot and Daumier, Manet and Toulouse-Lautrec. To the present generation, however, mention of Avignon means the festival. The festival of dramatic art that takes place annually between mid-July and mid-August enjoys tremendous interest and popularity. Throughout the summer months there are spectacles of *son et lumière*, giving another, ethereal quality to the Palace of the Popes.

The secular architecture has been less well preserved than the religious. However, in the old quarter there are medieval dwellings and mansions. These are particularly noticeable in the Rue Banasterie close to the cathedral (*banastes*, in Provençal, meaning basket makers), the Rue du Roi Réné and the Rue du Four. Down beside the river, the Rue des Teinturies retains all its ancient atmosphere, paved with pebbles and shaded by plane trees. The heart of the city is the Place de l'Horloge, an immense square shaded by plane trees and surrounded by the terraces of cafés.

The town's prosperity continued long after the departure of the Popes and Cardinals. In the seventeenth and eighteenth centuries splendid mansions were built in the Grand Rue, the prosperity continued until the Revolution.

All these medieval streets lead down to the Pont Saint Benezet, the far-famed Pont d'Avignon, although the dancing took place beneath and not upon it, in the shade of the arches. Legend relates that a shepherd boy named Benezet saw the bridge in a dream and heard voices bidding him to have it built. After submitting to various proofs of his good faith, both secular and religious, he

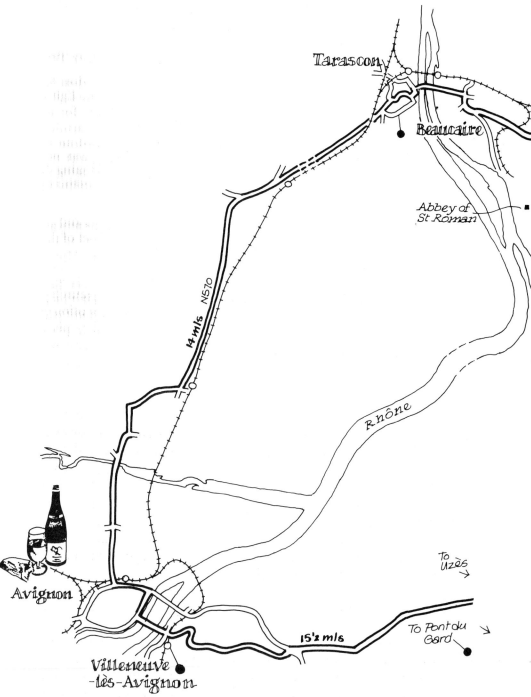

Tarascon

Beaucaire

Abbey of
St Roman

N570
14 mls

Rhône

Avignon

Villeneuve
-lès-Avignon

To
Uzès

To Pont du
Gard

15½ mls

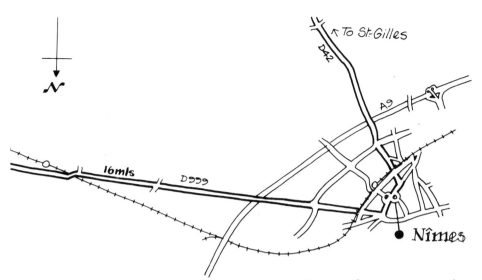

convinced an order of monks who collected offerings for its construction. Benezet was canonized in the twelfth century and a little chapel was erected to him on the second pier. The bridge, which is 900 meters long, used to lead to Villeneuve-lès-Avignon. Only four of the original twenty-two arches remain.

Lunch at the **Auberge de France**, Avignon.

Tarascon

Leaving Avignon on the N570 brings us to Tarascon, the derivation of whose name goes back nearly two millenia to when a legendary dragon, Tarasque, was raging through the countryside. Martha, who was evangelising here, overcame the monstrous beast by making the sign of the cross. Docile, it was captured. To commemorate this miracle, in 1474, the *Bon Roi Réné*, as this popular count of Provence was always called, organised large scale celebrations, and the legend is still fêted on the last Sunday of June when a giant effigy of the Tarasque is paraded through the streets, its jaws and tail kept in constant motion by boys in its interior.

On the left bank of the Rhône, and an important river port in the Middle Ages, Tarascon is dominated by the imposing mass of a great stronghold. Begun in the twelfth century on the site of a Roman fort, its building lasted for nearly three centuries, one of the finest feudal castles in the country. It belonged to the counts of Toulouse and suffered frequent sieges during the crusade against the Albigensians. It is in two parts, the lower courtyard, protected by

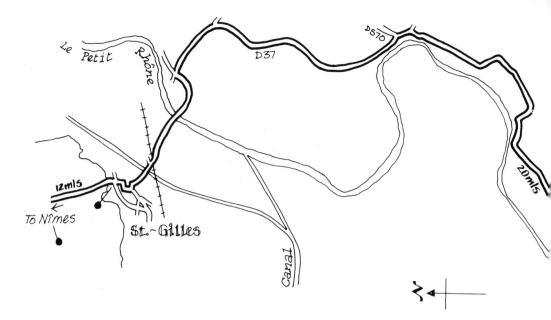

rectangular towers, and the immense seignorial dwelling, where the apartment of the Roi Réné is built round the court of honour, with vaulted ceilings and richly sculptured decoration. There are also two chapels, superimposed, the upper one with the oratories for the king and queen, the lower for the staff and court. From the terrace there is a fine view across the river to Beaucaire and over the hills. The church, founded in the tenth century and rebuilt in the twelfth, is dedicated to St. Martha for she was buried here. The seventeenth-century Hotel de Ville has a finely sculptured façade, decorated with a stone balcony. Today the town's chief interest is on market days, being an important centre for fruit and vegetables. Les Halles, as the immense covered market is called, is close to the suspension bridge across which is the rival town of Beaucaire, also built on a cliff.

Beaucaire

The rivalry in the past was when the Rhône served as frontier between Provence and Languedoc, each had a fortified castle facing across the river. Beaucaire still has a magnificent triangular keep, almost intact. Beaucaire Town Hall, built to the plans of Mansard, is a fine seventeenth-century monument, while the Church of Nôtre-Dame des Pommiers has a very beautiful façade.

For six centuries the fair at Beaucaire had world wide celebrity, merchants of every kind came from as far as Genoa and Malaga, Constantinople and

44

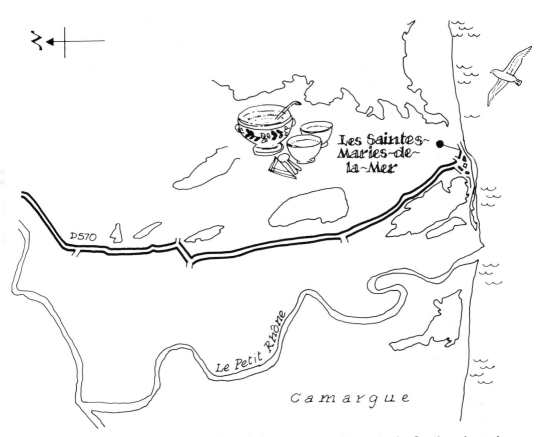

Hamburg. Its days were numbered, however, as the arrival of rail and road transport replaced the importance of traffic on the Rhône. Today the *pré* (or meadow) which was the site of the immense fair ground at the foot of the castle seems to serve principally for games of *boules* beneath its six hundred plane trees. It comes alive again only in mid-July when a fair is held there.

There are a number of fine old mansions in the Rue de la Republique, particularly noticeable being no. 23 where two magnificent stone figures guard the entrance, supporting a wrought-iron balcony. The street leads into the Place de la Republique, familiarly known as the Place Vieille since it is the oldest in the town. Its atmosphere might come straight out of Pagnol, the Beaucairois, as they sip their Pastis usually discuss the *taureaux*, for the veritable stars of Beaucaire are the bulls. The bull races are of three kinds: *L'abrivado* which takes place through the streets, followed by the guardians. The skill is to try to induce a bull to escape down a sidestreet out of the guardian's control. Next is the *encierro*, where the bulls are let loose in an enclosure, their horns enveloped in leather to make them safe. Lastly, the *cocarde*, where the competitors have to snatch the *cocarde* or rosettes which are tied to the animal's head. These performances take place in the arenas which were built in 1850, but it is recorded that even in Roman times the gladiators used to fight bulls here, in a circle formed by carts.

A little over two miles outside the town is the curious abbey of St. Roman, a twelfth-century chapel carved out of the rock which holds the saint's tomb. From the terrace above there is a splendid view over the Rhône.

Nîmes

Fifteen miles west brings us to Nîmes called, with good reason, the Rome of France. The most ancient of all the Roman cities of Gaul, it has preserved a remarkable assemblage of ancient monuments rivalling in number and beauty those of Arles and Rome. After his victory in Egypt over Anthony and Cleopatra, Octavius, who became the Emperor Augustus, granted to his veterans land around Nemausus as Nîmes was then called.

What epitomises the city above all else, I think, is the Maison Carrée, strangely named since it is by no means square, a marvellous temple built in honour of

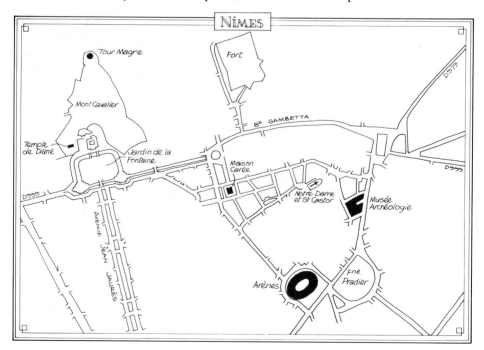

the grandson of Augustus. The purity of its form and the beautiful sculpture of its Corinthian columns show how strongly Roman architecture was influenced by the Greek. Built in the early years of the first century, it probably overlooked the Forum. With all the different uses to which the Maison Carrée was submitted, it is a miracle that the temple suffered so little, serving in turn as the Town Hall, a private dwelling and even as stables. Louis XIV gave permission to the Augustin monks for it to serve as their church. So great was its reputation from the Middle Ages onwards that the Minister Colbert contemplated transferring it, brick by brick, to Versailles. At the time of the Revolution it was bought as a national monument. Today it houses a museum of antiquity, among which are mosaics and friezes, a splendid head of Apollo in bronze and one of Venus in white marble.

Les Arènes, as the great amphitheatre is called, is almost a twin of that at Arles, holding over twenty thousand spectators. If not the largest of all these ancient amphitheatres, it is the best preserved despite having been transformed into a fortress in the fifth century by the invading Visigoths and later used to house a whole district of the town. It was not until the nineteenth century that it was finally liberated, cleared of the tons of debris and restored. At Whitsun and from June until September bull-fights are held here.

Of great interest, too, are the partly ruined temple of Diana, which dates to an earlier period, and the Magne tower where a staircase of a hundred and forty steps leads up to a platform which commands a really splendid view of the city and across to the hills. The Porte d'Auguste was part of the fortifications that were constructed between the years 1 and 15 B.C. Another pride of Nîmes, although of a much later date, are the ancient thermes, situated at the foot of a hill called the Mont Cavalier, which in the eighteenth century were skilfully transformed into gardens. They now rank among the most beautiful in France.

Time should be taken, too, to wander through the old quarter of picturesque streets huddled around the cathedral. The cathedral itself, Nôtre-Dame St. Castor, begun in the eleventh century, displays a mixture of styles having been frequently reconstructed. The façade has a frieze depicting figures from the Old Testament: Adam and Eve and Cain and Abel among them.

For those with the time there are first class museums in Nîmes, otherwise travel directly south to les Saintes-Maries-de-la-Mer.

Dinner and overnight at **Mas Sainte Hélène**, les Saintes-Maries-de-la-Mer.

Auberge de France
28 Place Horloge
Avignon
Tel: (90) 82 58 86

This centrally located restaurant — with a Michelin star — has a number of specialities, including delicious patisseries and excellent wines. Their Châteauneuf-du-Pape is particularly to be recommended.

Closed: 17 June to 4th July; 9 January to 1st February
Credit cards: American Express, Diner's Club, Eurocard, Visa

NIMES: USEFUL INFORMATION

Tourist Office: 6 Rue Auguste
                 Tel: (66) 67 29 11
Population: 129924
Altitude: 39 metres
Facilities: Airport, railway and coach stations,
                 hotels, swimming pools, skating rink,
                 golf course

Mas Sainte Helène
Stes.-Maries-de-la-Mer
Tel: (90) 47 83 29

Situated just a mile north of the town, this comfortable modern small hotel has an unsurpassed view over the Camargue.

Closed: 2nd January to 15th February
Rooms: 15
Facilities: Restaurant, private beach half a mile away, car park
Food: Seafood a speciality
Rating: ★★

**STES.-MARIES-DE-LA-MER: USEFUL
INFORMATION**

Tourist Office: Av. Van Gogh
                 Tel: (90) 47 82 55
Population: 2045
Facilities: 3 star municipal camping site with
                 restaurant

DAY 3

Les Saintes-Maries-de-la-Mer to Les Baux-de-Provence: approx. 35 miles.

For those with the time a twenty-mile detour westwards takes us through the Camargue, one of the most curious regions of France, to the crusader fortress town of Aigues-Mortes.

Otherwise, one should strike north from Saintes-Maries-de-la-Mer to Arles, an endearing old city which seems content to dream of her past glory, but is rich in ancient monuments.

After completing the visit of Arles we continue north by Fontvieille and Alphonse Daudet's celebrated hilltop windmill, to the marvellously situated Les Baux-de-Provence.

Travels in Provence

Breakfast at Les Saintes-Maries-de-la-Mer.

Time should be taken to explore Les Saintes-Maries-de-la-Mer. It is one of the oldest pilgrimage centres of France, supposedly dating back to the year 40 A.D. when tradition relates that Mary Jacobaeus, the sister of the Virgin, Mary Salome, the mother of the apostles John and James, their negro servant, Sarah, Lazarus who was raised from the dead, and his two sisters Mary Magdalene and Martha, Maximinus and Sidoine were cast out to sea by the Jews of Jerusalem in a ship without oars or sails.

By Divine Providence the ship landed on the beach which the present church of the Saintes-Maries overlooks. According to legend, after building a simple oratory dedicated to the Virgin, the little group then separated, Martha to evangelise Tarascon, Mary Magdalene to Ste. Baume, Lazarus to Marseilles and Maximinus and Sidoine to Aix, while the two Marys and Sarah remained at what is now called Les Saintes-Maries. When they died their relics were placed in the oratory and very soon pilgrims were coming here, most numerous of whom were nomads and gypsies who especially venerated Sarah. In the ninth century the church that replaced the oratory was fortified and formed part of the ramparts until the twelfth century when the present church was built on the same site, the crypt supposedly shelters the bones of the two Marys and Sarah.

To be there at the time of the pilgrimage is a memorable experience when, on May 24th and 25th and on the Saturday and Sunday closest to October 22nd, gypsies from throughout western Europe unite to honour their patron saint. On the first day the relics are brought down from the high chapel to the choir and the gypsies parade the statue of Sarah, richly adorned, down to the sea. Next day the statues are processed through the streets, along the beaches and into the sea. In the evening, after Vespers, the relics are returned to their chapel. This spontaneous outburst is at once fête and pilgrimage, with the guardians from the Camargue, the Arlesiennes in their national costume, the *farandoles* and *ferrades*, horse races and bull fights, a highly coloured spectacle.

Detour

To reach Aigues-Mortes one crosses the Camargue, one of the most curious regions of all France consisting of low-lying ground cut through with branches of the Rhône that flow through marshes and innumerable ponds. Rice-growing here has become an important source of revenue for the country, although for the visitor the chief interest are the grey horses, said to be descended from an Arab

St. Trophime — Arles

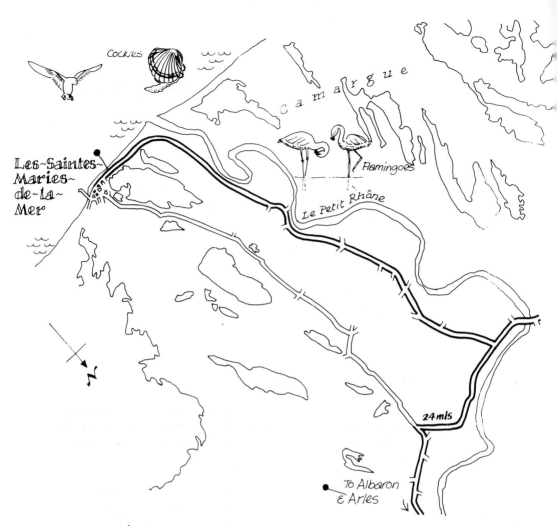

Detour contd.

race of the Saracens, and the herds of bulls destined for the ring. All watched over by guardians. Visitors can watch the *ferrades*, when the young bulls are separated and branded, the ceremony is followed by a bull fight. This national park, covering some forty-five thousand acres, is a paradise of wild life as well as an important botanical reserve. Thousands of birds of all species flock here including, most colourful of all, the marvellous pink flamingoes. In this part of Provence one seems always to be talking in superlatives, but the crusader fortress town of Aigues-Mortes, set among swamps and salines (salt beds), is one of the most striking existing examples of military architecture.

It was known as the town of St. Louis because, although the enthusiasm of the first four crusades had faded, Louis was a convinced crusader and during a severe illness he made a vow to take the Cross. Since there was no port on the

52

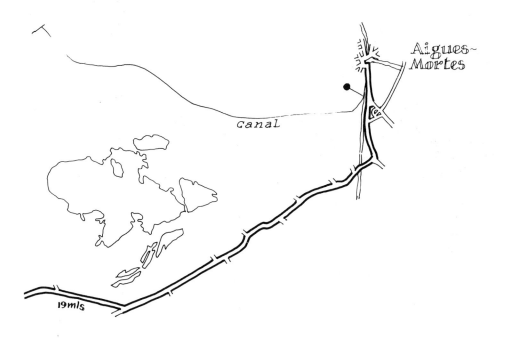

Mediterranean belonging to the Crown and he was disinclined to disembark from that of one of his subjects, he obtained from the monks of the Abbey of Psalmody this territory where there was already a small borough joined to the sea by a narrow channel and which he quickly developed into a fine port. In the year 1248 thirty-eight vessels set out, ships of no small importance since each could carry up to eight hundred crusaders and a hundred horses.

He reached Damiette, marched on Cairo and advanced as far as Mansourah. There, imprudence on the part of the avant garde led to complete confusion and the King was taken prisoner. So admired was he by the Moslems that he was often chosen to judge in their disputes and named *le Sultan Juste*. Upon his return to France he devoted himself to good works, built hospitals and founded convents. But despite having worshipped in Jerusalem, in 1270 he organised another, the eighth, crusade and although he was in very poor health the fatal expedition set off again from Aigues-Mortes, in the direction of Tunis. The plague ravaged his army and Louis died after caring for many other sufferers.

As one wanders through its silent streets, entered by the Porte de la Gardette which defended the town from the north, it is easy to imagine the scene as the crusaders left for the Holy Land. The crenellated ramparts are some of the most perfect still standing, surrounded by twenty towers, of which the most important is the Tour de Constance, a formidable keep. Here one sees the Salle de Gardes where the immense oven for baking bread is preserved, a tiny oratory set in the wall, and the Salle des Chevaliers where a number of celebrated prisoners were

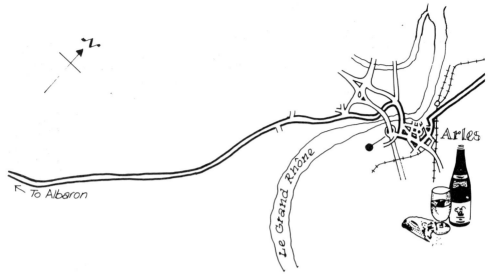

held, including Templars, Huguenots and Camisards. The motto 'Resist' which they carved in the wall can still be seen. One can also make the rounds of the ramparts, looking down on what was once an immense moat protecting the town. Today it is no more than a swamp for with the silting up of the port the town's prosperity lasted only until the fourteenth century. Visits to the Salines can be organised from July 1st until August 31st on Tuesdays and Thursdays by applying to the Tourist Office.

Arles

Those not visiting Aigues-Mortes will strike directly north for Arles. The twenty-one mile stretch of road passes through Albaron, once fortified but of which only the thirteenth-century tower remains. Then, after the vast, solitary expanse one enters Arles by crossing the Rhône, for here the river divides into two arms before reaching the sea.

The Boulevard Lices, where I recommend lunch at the **Lou Marquès**, is one of the most animated in the city, a favourite with Arlesians, its broad pavements shaded by plane trees and lined with café terraces. Called by a Latin poet 'the little Rome of the Gauls', by a Bordelais poet 'the queen of the Gauls', Arles seems still content to dream of her past glory. Although reputed to have been founded by Phoenician Greeks in the sixth century B.C., it was not until the advent of the Romans that her real importance began.

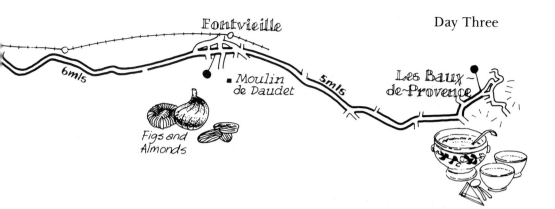

Fontvieille

Moulin de Daudet

6mls

5mls

Les Baux-de-Provence

Figs and Almonds

From earliest times she owed her great economic growth to the Rhône. As an inland port Arles was so celebrated for her ship building that Caesar had a dozen galleys built here for his attack on Marseilles which, at that time, was supporting Pompey. After his victory Caesar made her a Roman colony, one of the highest honours, and her port became afloat with ships from all over the world. Her apogee, however, came four centuries later at the time of the Emperor Constantine who renamed her Constantina, the capital of Gaul. As well as her political and administrative rôle, in the fifth century Arles became a bishopric as well, and in the sixth century was given the title of 'religious metropolis', a number of ecclesiastical synods being held here. When, in the ninth century, Arles became the capital of the Burgundian kingdom of Arelet, she had already declined considerably as a result of continual invasions from both Barbarians and Saracens, but remained a city republic until 1251 when she was annexed by the Count of Provence and became no more than a provincial town, replaced by Aix politically and by Marseilles economically. So long as the navigation on the Rhône flourished she managed to keep fairly busy, but the arrival of the railway was fatal so that today her only importance is as an agricultural centre.

Epitomising antiquity, the old city is now one vast museum. The hub of the city is the Place de la Republique, in the centre of which is an obelisk brought here from the Roman theatre, where it used to mark the finishing point for chariot races. It is set on a pedestal in a pool of water, in the form of four leaves, which sparkles with darting goldfish. Facing the obelisk is the imposing seventeenth-century Hotel de Ville, surmounted by a bronze figure of Mars dating from 1570. It was built by Mansart who was one of the principle architects of Versailles, his style is evident in the high windows, the moulding and love of sculpture.

Nearby are two churches, those of St. Trophime and St. Anne. That of St. Anne has been disaffected and now houses the Musée Lapidaire, or museum of pagan art. This very rich collection includes mosaics and sarcophagi, friezes and altars to Apollo, statues and a bust of Constantine II, son of Constantine the Great. There is also a fine collection of Greek and Etruscan pottery and an interesting room of prehistory.

The Musée d'Art Chrétien, housed in the ancient Jesuit chapel, is also well worth a visit with a superb collection of marble sarcophagi of the fourth and fifth centuries. In the showcases the evolution of pottery techniques in the Roman Empire can be studied as well as a full set of coins struck at Arles from the reign of Constantine the Great to the Middle Ages. The Musée Reattu, housed in a former fifteenth-century Commandary of the Order of Malta displays a fine series of sixteenth-century Arras tapestries and numerous paintings of the French, Italian and Dutch schools. Lastly, and above all not to be missed, is the Museon Arlaten, the Arlesien museum which was founded by the poet Mistral who endowed it with the hundred thousand gold francs that he received as his Nobel Prize.

Some thirty rooms are consecrated mainly to the region of Arles: furniture and ceramics, costumes and trades, but of particular interest is the way that it illustrates the everyday life in Provence, with scenes portraying such occasions as Christmas Eve, with the grandfather pouring the new wine on the flaming logs in the hearth.

To return to the marvellous cathedral of St. Trophime which is one of the finest of all the Romanesque monuments in Provence: St Trophime was a Greek bishop who evangelised Provence and the present church is built over an earlier one, probably of Carolingian origin. The sumptuously carved monumental doorway is alive with groups of figures: Christ and the apostles, scenes from the Last Judgment, from the Nativity, saints and guardian angels, making it a masterpiece of Provençal Romanesque art. The interior is equally impressive. The nave, luminous with light from the high windows, displays a Romanesque sobriety in contrast to the beautiful, but ornate, decoration of the Gothic choir. On the south side of the cathedral a staircase leads up to the cloister, one of the most celebrated in all France. The south and west sides are Gothic, the north and east Romanesque and the angle pillars, copied from antique models, and the historiated capitals show how great were the decorative powers of the Provençal school. Above all one is struck by the silence, for this cloister, right in the city centre, possesses a unique quality of tranquillity.

Close to the vestiges of the ancient forum is the Place Frederic Mistral with a handsome statue of the poet which he himself inaugurated not long before his death. Then, after a huddle of narrow streets, one comes upon a high railing which guards the great expanse where once stood Constantine's Palace. All that remains now are the thermes, a vast building in red brick, the largest in Provence. Apart from the ramparts, the principle interest of Roman Arles are the Arènes, the Theatre Antique and the Alyscamps.

The Arènes, or amphitheatre, was set up in the second century A.D. and could hold twenty-five thousand spectators. In the eleventh century it was turned into a fortress, enclosing a whole district of the town including two churches, and it was restored during the last century. Fully to appreciate the tremendous dimensions of the amphitheatre one should go up to the platform of the tower

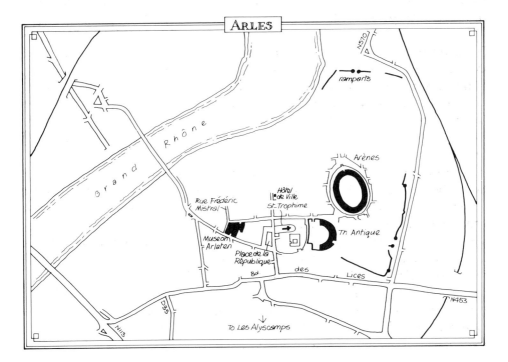

from where there is also a wide view over the Rhône, the Alpilles and the Abbey of Montmajour. This great amphitheatre is still very much alive when it rings to the 'vivas' of an excited public during the corridas which take place at Whitsun and during the summer months.

Only a step away, the once vast Theatre Antique has a sorrier history for, in order to build the cathedral of St. Trophime, it was disgracefully plundered, serving as little more than a quarry. Two beautiful marble columns remain and row upon row of stone seats reach up the hillside. But all that was of architectural interest was taken to the museum of pagan art, leaving, scattered among the grasses, mutilated statues watched over by the great cypresses above. Nevertheless, each year, at the end of June and of July, theatre reviews take place and the youth of Arles awaken the desolation with their *farandoles*.

Close to the Boulevard des Lices, the Alyscamps, from Roman times until the Middle Ages, was one of the most famed Christian cemeteries in the world; the dead were brought from far and wide to this ground that was hallowed by the tomb of St. Honoratus. But this once sacred spot suffered no better than the Theatre Antique, for at the time of the Renaissance the seigneurs of Arles adopted the profoundly sacrilegious habit of offering to their important guests the most finely sculptured of the sarcophagi from the cemetery. While the monks, in whose charge it lay, used the stones of the ancient tombs to build their churches, convents and even to adorn their gardens. Fortunately the museum of Christian art managed to rescue a few admirable pieces which at least give one an idea of the past splendour of the Alyscamps. There also remains the impressive avenue of poplars, bordered with empty sarcophagi of no artistic interest, and ruined chapels, which leads to an empty church.

Nearer our own times, Van Gogh was intoxicated by the luminosity of the countryside around Arles which he painted unceasingly from 1888–1890, three hundred canvases, among which were the Alyscamps, the house of Van Gogh, l'Arlesienne and Barques sur la Plage, and the Bridge of Langlois. It was while he was living here with Gaughin that he cut off his ear, but the house where he lodged was destroyed during the last war.

The women of Arles are reputed to be the most beautiful of France, the 'pale and beautiful Arlesienne' as Jules Michelet calls her, conjuring up an image of charm and mystery, epitomised when she wears the national dress.

Fontvieille

Arles is only five miles from Fontvieille, and the hilltop windmill from which Alphonse Daudet dated his celebrated 'Lettres de mon moulin'. In fact, Daudet wrote his stories in Paris, and when he was at Fontvieille it was with friends at the Château de Montauban that he used to stay, but he loved to idle at the mill, listening to the miller, and strolling over the hillside.

Although the interior is now a museum and the sails no longer turn, his spell remains in the isolation of the plain where the only sounds are the breeze whistling through the gorse.

Down in the village there is no great religious monument, no princely castle, but a village of some three thousand inhabitants where the gardens are shaded by fig and almond trees, colourful with hollyhocks and oleander. On the western edge of the village stands a fourteenth-century tower, built with stones from the nearby quarries, which is supposed to connect by an underground passage with the castle of Montmajour. On Christmas Eve a Provençal mass for the shepherds is held in the little church.

Les Baux-de-Provence

Les Baux-de-Provence is yet another place which can only be described in superlatives. Amidst wild and grandiose scenery, the village is perched on rocky cliffs, a setting beloved by artists. Inevitably there are also souvenir shops and coachloads of tourists, for one must share the uniqueness of Les Baux with her thousands of other admirers.

Today half-ruined, in the Middle Ages it was of great importance, seat of the powerful warlords, the Counts of Baux. Mistral described them as 'a race of eagles' and it was perhaps to justify this epithet that they claimed to have been descended from Balthazar, one of the three wise men. From the eleventh century they were among the most powerful feudal lords of the Midi, with seventy-nine boroughs depending on them.

Wandering through the old streets, one notices houses hewn out of rock, the stump of an ancient aquaduct and crumbling chapels until one comes to the ruins of the castle, high up on its mount, which held such brilliant court, particularly those courts of love, where Chivalry played a prominent role. The dungeons and ramparts all form part of the rock on which they were built from where there is a magnificent view over the Val d'Enfer whose twisted and contorted rocks, together with the curious effect left from the quarrying of bauxite out of the limestone, well justify the description, valley of Hell. Bauxite, the mineral that is essential for aluminium, was first discovered here in 1822 and owes its name to the village.

Back in the village, a visit should be made to the little Romanesque church of St. Vincent, with its elegant *lanterne des morts*. New chapels were added in later years, carved out of the rock, while the stained glass windows were painted by the modern artist, Max Ingrand.

To participate in Midnight Mass on Christmas Eve crowds come from all the surrounding district celebrating the *fête des bergers*. The shepherds in their flowing cloaks, to the accompaniment of flutes and drums, process to the church with a cart, drawn by a ram, containing a lamb, which they present as their offering. At the foot of the castle is the Oustaù de Baumanière.

Dinner and overnight at the **Oustaù de Baumanière**, Les Baux-de-Provence.

Lou Marquès
Boulevard des Lices
Arles
Tel: (90) 93 43 20

An excellent restaurant — with a Michelin star — where you can enjoy such specialities as *Magret de canard aux picholines* and a delicious *Gratin aux oranges*. Its recommended wines are the local Côteaux de Baux.

Closed: Beginning of November to 22nd December
Credit cards: American Express, Diner's Club, Eurocard, Visa

ARLES: USEFUL INFORMATION	
Tourist Office:	Esplanade des Lices
	Tel: (90) 96 29 35
Population:	50772
Altitude:	9 metres
Facilities:	Railway station

Oustaù de Baumanière
Les Baux-de-Provence
Tel: (90) 54 33 07

This hotel-restaurant is one of the most celebrated in France. It is an ancient Provençal *mas* with splendid arched stone ceilings and massive fireplaces. The tone has also been maintained throughout the interior with antique furniture and paintings.

Closed:	16th January to 1st March
Rooms:	14, and 11 apartments
Facilities:	Bar, restaurant, swimming pool, tennis courts and car park
Credit cards:	American Express, Diner's Club, Eurocard, Visa
Food:	Having 3 Michelin stars it is one of the gastronomic shrines of France — with an exquisite *Souflée de homard* as well as other specialities.
Wine:	Gigondas and Côteaux de Baux
Rating:	★★★★★

LA CABRO D'OR
Les Baux-de-Provence
Tel: (90) 54 33 21

A charming and very comfortable Provençal inn, very quiet with a pleasant terrace.

Closed:	15th November to 20th December
Rooms:	Restaurant, bar, swimming pool, tennis courts
Credit cards:	American Express, Diner's Club, Eurocard, Visa
Food:	With a Michelin star, an excellent meal is assured. Specialities include *Filet de Loup en papillote*, and *Noisettes d'agneau*.
Wine:	Gigondas and Côteaux de Baux
Rating:	★★★

LES BAUX-DE-PROVENCE: USEFUL INFORMATION

Tourist Office:	Impasse du Château (open Easter to October) Tel: (90) 97 34 39
Population:	433
Altitude:	280

Nôtre-Dame de la Garde — Marseilles

DAY 4

From Les Baux-de-Provence to Aubagne: approx. 92 miles.

From Les Baux it is only five miles to St. Rémy-de-Provence and the marvellous ruins of Glanum. After exploring this enchanting little town we cross the Alpilles to Salon-de-Provence. Those with the time can continue due south across the plain of Crau, working round by Martigues to Marseilles. Those more pressed for time can take the road direct to Marseilles where there is much to visit. Eight miles from Marseilles is Aubagne, associated, above all, with Marcel Pagnol.

Breakfast at Les Baux-de-Provence.

St. Rémy-de-Provence

Take the D27 to St. Rémy-de-Provence, a typical little Provençal town surrounded by olive and almond groves, oaks and cypresses. Archeologists from all over the world take the broad avenue, shaded by plane trees, that leads to the once prosperous Gallo-Roman city of Glanum, that was almost totally destroyed by barbarian invasions in the third century. It is indeed one of the most moving sights in Provence. Known as the Antiques, the most celebrated monument is the admirable mausoleum, raised in honour of the grandsons of Augustus and one of the most beautiful in the Roman world as well as being one of the best preserved. It comprises two storeys, the first set on four pillars resting on a stone pedestal decorated and crowned by a cupola.

Although the nearby Arc de Triomph is badly ruined, one can still appreciate the perfection of its proportions. Not far away lie whole streets where the foundations of private houses and public edifaces that formed this Gallo-Roman town of the 1st century have been excavated, as well as thermes, the forum, canalisations and an elegant vasque, or fountain. There are also remains of the Gallo-Greek settlement dating back to the second century B.C. The discovery of this earlier city has thrown fresh light on the importance of the colony.

Back in St. Rémy, the fifteenth-century Hôtel de Sade has a fine collection of varied artifacts coming mostly from the excavations at Glanum. Also to be visited is the church of the ancient priory of St. Pol-de-Mausole with its beautiful little Romanesque cloister. Now serving as an asylum, it was here than Van Gogh spent a year after his first attack of madness and where he painted some of his finest masterpieces.

In the Rue Hoche stands the house where Nostradamus, the famous astrologer, was born in 1503. His prophecies, arranged into ten centuries, are still studied today. Not everyone realises, however, that it was as a doctor, whose skill did much to arrest the plague raging at the time, that Nostradamus first became known. His prophecies brought him into favour with Catherine de Medici and among his other powers he was supposed to have supplied her with the poisons which she used so skilfully in disposing of her enemies. When her son, Henri II, was killed in a tournament and it was found that this had been predicted by Nostradamus, his fame was established.

In the old town are numerous cafés with terraces stretching onto the pavement, 'The Regence' being considered the most classic and 'les Arts' the most chic. St. Rémy has always been popular with artists and writers who would gather to converse interminably on these terraces and the names of some of the restaurants bear witness: the Van Gogh in the Avenue Jean Moulin and 'le jardin de Frédéric' in the Boulevard Gambetta. Frédéric, of course, being Frédéric Mistral who was born three miles away at the nearby village of Millaine. Gounod wrote his *mireille* here, drawn from Mistral's Mireio. The choice is wide, be it for a Pastis, a snack or a coffee.

Eyguières

Turn south following the N99, D24, D25 and D17 to the little-visited village of Eyguières, a small gem at the foot of the Alpilles, which takes its name from the numerous fountains fed from the streams which flow down from the hills. Its church has a splendid altar surrounded by six marble columns and a handsome organ.

Nearby are the picturesque ruins of Castellas de Roquemartine, built at different periods, whose seigneurs, though less well known than those of Les Baux, were nevertheless remembered for their welcoming of strangers to their brilliant court, fêted by troubadours and poets.

Salon-de-Provence

Continue along the D17 into Salon-de-Provence which, just south of the Alpilles, is like that region, impregnated with the spirit of Provence, surrounded by scrubland and olive groves. In fact, since the fifteenth century oil has been extracted from olives here, an industry that was further developed by the Minister Colbert. Today, it is still an important agricultural centre.

The old city of Salon is dominated by its Château de l'Emperi, the great residence of the Archbishops of Arles, and a splendid specimen of a fortified palace. It was begun as early as the tenth century and restored in the thirteenth and fifteenth. A vaulted passage leads to the Court of Honour, surrounded by

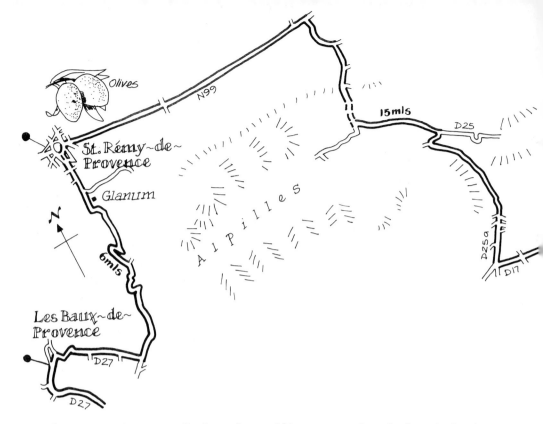

elegant Renaissance galleries. The twelfth-century chapel of St. Catherine as well as the Salle d'Honneur and twenty other rooms now house the Musée de l'Emperi, a marvel for those interested in armoury, from the reign of Louis XIV until 1918, arms and canons, uniforms and decorations, flags and pictures of every epoch, the Napoleonic period in particular. The Town Hall is in the gracious and harmonious style of the Grand Siècle, as the time of Louis XIV was called. In the centre of its square is a statue of the engineer Adam de Craponne who was responsible for the fertilisation of a large part of this region by constructing a canal to link its water with the river Durance. Better known, though certainly less materially useful to the inhabitants of Salon, is Nostradamus who lived here for the last seventeen years of his life. When he first arrived, it is recorded that he was overwhelmed by the grateful crowds who surrounded him. He was buried in the Gothic church of St. Laurent where his tomb, in one of the side chapels, is beside a handsome sixteenth-century alabaster statue of the Virgin.

Lunch at **Robin**, Salon-de-Provence.

Follow the autoroute, or the N113, south direct to Marseilles or, if you have extra time available take the following detour via Martigues.

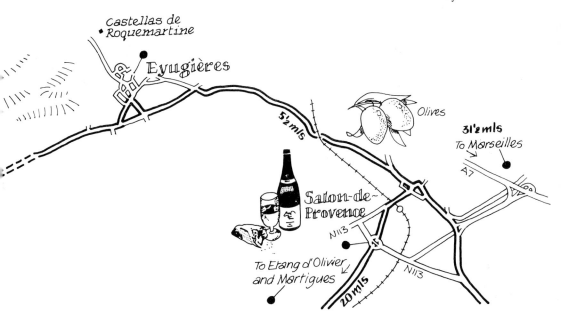

Detour

Salon in the past was known as Salon-de-Crau, and it is to the plain of Crau that we now turn, continuing down the N569. This great plain, which lies between the Alpilles, the Rhône and the sea, has always, like the great lonely expanse of the Camargue, caught the imagination. But, unlike the swamps of the Camargue, it used to consist of such a strange mixture of shingle and gravel that it was explained by a Greek legend whereby Hercules, on his way to Spain, encountered hostile Ligurian tribes here. Having exhausted his supply of arrows, he called upon Jupiter to help him, whereupon there descended a storm of stones and shingle which dispersed the enemy. Geologists explain it by the fact that the Durance, before being a tributary of the Rhône, used to flow directly into the sea, accumulating in its delta the stones washed down from the rocky banks. Today, partly due to the canal which the engineer Adam de Craponne constructed, it is fertile with fruit and vegetables, green with meadowland and one of the most important producers of fodder in the country. As one approaches Istres, one passes the Graeco-Ligurian oppidum of Castallan which dominates the Etang d'Olivier.

Istres, on the edge of the lake, has an interesting museum of history, prehistory, folklore and archeology and the flora and fauna of the region. Much of its archeological interest is due to the proximity of the important site of St. Blaise, close to the little twelfth-century chapel from which the site took its name. Excavations have revealed that the site was occupied from the years 49–7 B.C. by

Detour contd.

Phoceans, Greeks and Romans, abandoned and then inhabited again between the fifth and eleventh centuries of our era. The site is well worth visiting. Two miles further on, the little town of St. Mitre-les-Ramparts is still surrounded by its fifteenth-century fortifications, pierced by two gateways. A warren of narrow streets lead to the church, where there is a splendid view over the lake of Engrenier. Which brings us to Martigues, a distance of twenty-one miles from Salon-de-Provence. The character of this 'Venice of Provence', as Martigues is called, has fortunately not really suffered from being close to the gigantic industrial development of Fos. The present Martigues, linked by canals, consisted of three separate towns until 1581 when Ferrières, Jonquières and the Ile St. Genest became one community. The very name of Martigues seems to breathe the sun and sea, but it probably derived from Marthe, the Syrian priestess who accompanied the Roman general Marius.

Situated between the immense salt water lake of Berre and the canal which links it to the sea, it has always been primarily a little fishermen's village, where one can still be sure of finding a good *bouillabaisse*. Its heart is beside the canal of St. Sebastien. Like all fishermen, those of Martigues were always an independent race, but until the last century they had a particularity unique in France, a tribunal de Pêche which defended their rights.

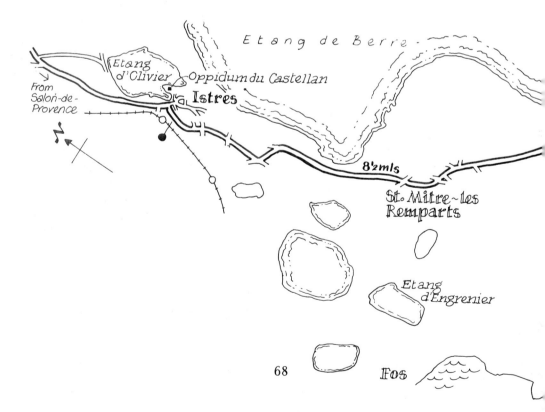

Detour contd.

For centuries they had to struggle against the privileges of the *bordigadiers*, who earned their living by planting *bordigues*, a kind of reed, in the muddy canals, joined together by stakes, to form a circle in which the fish were caught. This method was practised in all the canals except those of Pontet and St. Sebastien. Rivalry, of course, was ferocious between these *bordigadiers* and the fishermen, and a print in the Musée du Vieux Martigues shows very clearly the canals as they existed in the past.

As one explores the district of Ferrières one realises why it is so loved by artists. From the Pont Sebastien one looks over the colourful boats anchored along the canal, churches and houses reflected in its waters. This much-painted corner is known as *le miroir des oiseaux*.

The street names often indicate Martigues' past: the Rue Gatinière, so called because almost all the houses possessed courtyards in which they kept their chickens, the *galines*: the Rue des Fours and the Rue de la Chaine, because in the past a chain across the canal prevented boats entering without paying their dues. At the end of a narrow street one comes on a square shaded by plane trees, a fountain gushing out cool water. Here stands the seventeenth-century church of St Madeleine, looking out on *le miroir des oiseaux*. It has a fine façade in Corinthinian style, the inside is richly decorated and the organ is imposing. The Town Hall is of the same period. The Église de Ferrières was begun in the fourteenth century, while, higher up, the Chapelle de Nôtre-Dame de la

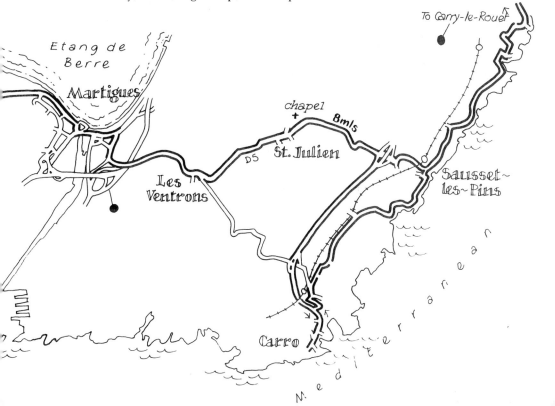

Detour contd.

Misericorde is known more usually as la Bonne Mère. On the way one passes the house of Charles Maurras, who was born here. Famous or infamous, no Frenchman can be ignorant of the importance of Maurras, both as writer and politician, Monarchist and anti-Dreyfusard. Napoleon, then Commandant of the Artillery and Inspector of the Fortresses, climbed to the top of the hill, after liberating Toulon, the seige where that great Corsican won his spurs.

This is the best possible view over Martigues, encompassing her canals and the Rhône delta. The district of Ferrières should not be left without a visit to the Musée du Vieux Martigues, housed in the seventeenth-century maison Maurel. The entrance hall is majestic with a beautiful wrought-iron staircase. There are many associations with fishing, models relating to the industry include a *marlussier*, the boat that brought back the cod from Newfoundland.

There is much, too, of archeological interest, with various objects excavated from the sites round Martigues. Nearby is the Musée Ziem, named after the nineteenth-century painter, which as well as a collection of Provençal painters has also a section of ethnography, archeology and prehistory. In the Jonquières, the southern district of Martigues, is the seventeenth-century church of St. Genes, in front of which stands the statue of Gerard Tenque, born in the eleventh century, who founded the Ordre des Hospitaliers de St. Jean de Jerusalem, who later became the Knights of Malta. Behind the church, the chapel of l'Annonciade was built in 1636 for the use of the Penitents Blancs. It is a beautiful little chapel, baroque in style, with a monumental, beautifully carved high altar. Walls and ceiling are also richly painted. One leaves Martigues on the D5 for Marseilles, a distance of twenty-two miles.

At Les Ventrons a two-mile detour could be made to the beautiful little Romanesque chapel of St. Julien where the Gallo-Roman bas-relief is one of the most important in France, dating from the 1st century. Set in the north wall of the chapel, it consists of eight figures, almost of full height, thought to represent two deceased surrounded by members of their family.

At the little fishing port of Carro one turns east, past the pleasant resort and fishing port of Sausset-les-Pins and Carry-le-Rouet, also a resort and port surrounded by pine trees; the little creek of le Rouet-Plage and Ensuès-la-Redonne, a village of vineyards.

Madrague-de-Gignac nestles at the end of a little calanque (or fjord), after which the scenery becomes more rugged, with rocks and an occasional pine, to l'Estaque, beloved by Cézanne when it was no more than a little fishing village, but which is now the biggest fishing port of Marseilles as well as a yacht harbour.

Marseilles

The regions visited so far would be difficult to reach without a car, but Marseilles can be reached either by plane or by the T.G.V. (Train Grand Vitesse) from Paris, after which trains run the whole way along the coast as far as Menton on the Italian frontier. Cars can be rented at the airport. And there is a good service of long distance coaches to Aix and Nîmes.

Marseilles is not only the second most important city of France but one of the greatest seaports of the world. Despite its size and bustle one cannot feel a stranger here, pulsating as it is with a medley of nationalities. Even for those who demur at the prospect of visiting this vast city, Marseilles is not to be missed.

From the earliest times its great port, in the Greek *Massalia*, was the legendary crossroads where civilisation met and mingled. Moreover, its history dates back over two thousand years to when, around 600 B.C. it was founded by Phocean immigrants from Asia Minor and soon became a prosperous trading place. The Massalians defended themselves successfully against the Carthaginians after calling in the aid of the Romans. Its cultural springs, too,

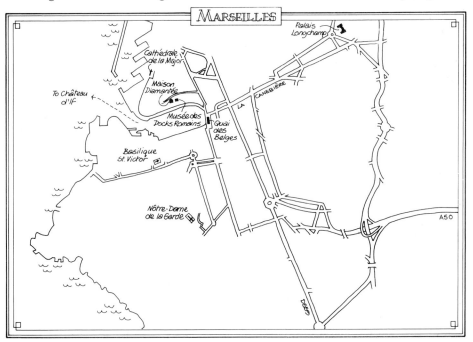

run deep, lauded by Pliny. Already, under the earlier emperors, it ranked as one of the great seats of learning, called by Cicero 'the Athens of Gaul'.

In 1947, when reconstruction work was underway, the remains were found of what may have been one of the oldest Greek ships ever discovered, dating from around 300 B.C., sunk deep in the Vieux Port, which was the original Greek harbour. The old harbour is still alive with activity, fishing boats and sailing craft glide in and out between the neo-classical forts of St. John and St. Nicolas which protect the entrance to the dock.

Like all cities of such commercial importance, Marseilles was embroiled in numerous disputes. During the Roman domination she backed Pompey against Caesar in the civil war. It was a bad choice resulting in a six month seige, and with Caesar's victory she lost much of her maritime importance. Sacked by barbaric invasions, her commercial activities were eclipsed until the time of the Crusades when her magnificent harbour furnished a much-needed maritime need and she flourished anew. In 1481, she was united to the French Crown with the rest of Provence.

Marseilles welcomed the Revolution and, as already mentioned, Mirabeau represented her, together with Aix, in the Third Estate. Although Roger de Lisle's famous anthem was composed at Strasbourg, it was first sung at Marseilles during a banquet in honour of the five hundred volunteers for Paris. So great was their enthusiasm for the theme that they sung it again and again, in their rich meriodinal accents, through the streets of the capital, thus it became known as the Marseillaise.

However pressed for time, a must for every visitor is to idle along the Canebière, the Champs-Elysée of Marseilles, harbouring some of the best

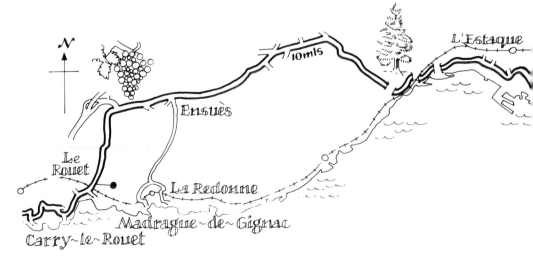

shopping outside the capital and stiff with cafés of all sorts and prices. For a quick round, you can take the no. 82 bus from the foot of the Canebière. It covers most of the city with some splendid views across to the islands from the Corniche President Kennedy, which stretches for three miles by the sea. One can take a boat trip around the harbour, where the Quai des Belges is the scene of a sprawling fish market. Excursion boats leave from here for the infamous Château d'If, built on a rock by François I as a prison, and immortalised by Dumas' *Count of Monte Cristo*.

Close to the port is the fine baroque Hotel de Ville, built in the seventeenth century. Nearby, in the Maison Diamantée, is housed the Musée du Vieux Marseille covering much of interest in Provençal life; furniture and objects of domestic use, earthenware and costumes; crêches and a fine collection of santons (see p. 84).

One must climb up to the basilica of Nôtre-Dame de la Garde, built in Roman-Byzantine style during the nineteenth century on the site of a thirteenth-century chapel that had been dedicated to Nôtre-Dame. The interior of the basilica, in marble of varying colours, has mosaics and mural paintings of the Dusseldorf school. While the crypt has a beautiful sculptured marble Mater Dolorosa. The steeple is surmounted by an enormous gilt statue of the Virgin who keeps eternal watch over the ancient city. From the terrace around the basilica one has an incomparable view over the mast-strewn harbour and an immense sea of tiled roofs below.

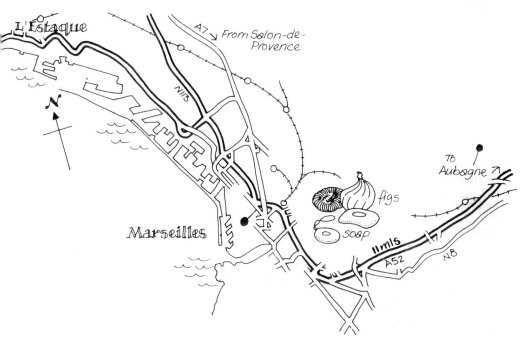

Fourteen hundred years separates the founding of Nôtre-Dame de la Garde and the fifth-century basilica of St. Victor, built to honour the third-century martyr. Almost completely destroyed by the Saracens, it was rebuilt in 1040 with frequent reconstruction over the centuries and strongly fortified. In fact, from the exterior, it resembles less an abbey than a powerful fortress.

Nearby is the Musée des Docks Romains which exhibits all that was found during the excavations in the old harbour in 1947. Among the city's notable monuments are the nineteenth-century Cathedral de la Major, a basilica in Byzantine style and close to the traces of the *ancienne Major*, the old Romanesque minster with a Renaissance chapel. Nearby, too, are the circular Chapelle du Calvaire and the Clocher des Accoules, the tower being all that remains of the twelfth-century church, one of the oldest in Marseilles. In the district of the Panier is the seventeenth-century Hospice de la Charité, and old, narrow streets with high houses, typical of Provence, colourful with lines of washing strung across.

The immense, Baroque Palais de Longchamps heavily sculptured and with monumental fountains, is linked by an archway to the Musée des Beaux-Arts where many of the great artists are represented. Mention, too, should be made of the blocks of modern flats, seventeen storeys high, known as Unité d'Habitation which were designed by Corbusier in 1952.

Aubagne

Aubagne, eight miles east of Marseilles, would be a good stop for the night. Dinner and overnight at the **Hostellerie Manon des Sources**, Aubagne.

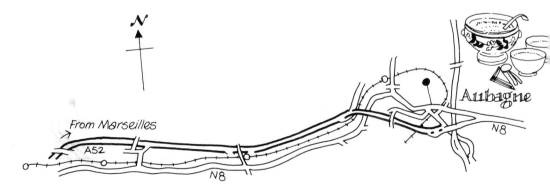

Robin
1 Boulevard G.-Clemenceau
Salon-de-Provence
Tel: (90) 56 06 53

A pleasant restaurant with a Michelin star where the specialities include a delectable *Civet de homard* and a marvellous trolley of desserts. Meyreuil wine makes a good accompaniment.

Closed: February
Credit cards: American Express, Diner's Club, Eurocard, Visa

SALON-DE-PROVENCE: USEFUL INFORMATION

Tourist Office: 56 Cours Gimon
                 Tel: (90) 56 27 60
Population: 35845
Altitude: 82 metres
Facilities: Golf course

Hostellerie Manon des Sources
Aubagne
Tel: (42) 03 10 31

A very quiet hotel two miles outside Aubagne (D44).

Rooms: 20
Facilities: Restaurant, meals served on the terrace, swimming pool, tennis
                courts, car park
Credit cards: American Express, Diner's Club, Visa
Food: A very good choice offered
Rating: ★★

MARSEILLES: USEFUL INFORMATION

Tourist Office: 4 Canebière 13001
                 Tel: (91) 54 91 11
Population: 878689
Facilities: Airport, railway
                 station, golf course

AUBAGNE: USEFUL INFORMATION

Tourist Office: Esplanade Gen.-de-
                 Gaulle
                 Tel: (42) 03 49 98
Population: 38571
Altitude: 102 metres

Aix-en-Provence

DAY 5

Aubagne to Brignoles: approx. 60 miles.

After visiting Aubagne, a detour can be made to the Calanques and the coast as far as Sanary. Otherwise we turn due north to Aix-en-Provence, no doubt one of the most beautiful of cities. Those with the time can continue north to the hills of the Luberon and the old, very Provençal towns of Apt and Manosque. Back in Aix another alternative is the round of the Montagne Ste.-Victoire.

Otherwise, one should turn east on the motorway to St. Maximin-Ste.-Baume and the immense range of the Ste. Baume, one of the greatest high places in the country. Another well worthwhile detour is fifteen miles north to Barjoles. Otherwise, continue along the motorway to Brignoles.

Breakfast at Aubagne.

A short visit should be made to Aubagne, situated in a green valley and looking across to the range of the Etoile, the little Alps of Provence. A fortified borough in the past, there remain only a few traces of her ancient ramparts and a twelfth-century church, restored in the seventeenth century. Since 1962 Aubagne has been the headquarters of the French Foreign Legion, before that stationed in Algeria, and the Musée de la Legion Etrangère has an interesting collection of documents, uniforms and souvenirs of the Legion's most important members.

The principle association of Aubagne, however, is with Marcel Pagnol, author, poet, cineaste and member of the French Academy. He was born here in 1895 at no. 16, Rue de la Cour Barthélémy. Traditionally, the local craft has always been ceramics, and its artists have created the delightful 'Petit monde de Marcel Pagnol' in a series of santons illustrating his most popular works.

Detour

Those with the time would do well to continue south to the Calanques, whose rocky cliffs plunge down almost vertically. These narrow fjords, which penetrate sometimes as much as a mile inland, are unique in France. For a long time they could not be reached by road at all. Now that of Port-Miou can be reached from Cassis by car, a distance of two miles, or else (but this means more walking) one can take the D559 from Cassis, turning left into a narrow road through the forest of la Gardiole as far as the Col de la Gardiole where there is a car park. From there it is about an hour's walk to the Calanque d'En Vau, the most celebrated and impressive of the three, with rocks and a tiny beach.

Alternatively, there are boat excursions from Cassis which take less than an hour there and back, certainly the least time consuming way of seeing them.
Cassis, thirteen miles from Aubagne, for long remained a little fishing village, since tourists tended to go further east. Today, like everywhere along this coast, it is better to go there out of season. It is indeed an attractive resort, surrounded by mountains and with three little rock-bound bays. The old town has all the attributes of the picturesque, remaining very largely eighteenth-century, its heart is the Place Baragon.

As a fishing port it is still important, its fish are considered to be of a very fine quality and there is plenty of seafood. Oursins, or sea-urchins, for those who have acquired their very special taste, marry marvellously with the white wine of Cassis which comes from the vineyards of the surrounding hills. The great Provençal poet, Mistral, talked often of these wines in his poems and even addressed the following flattering autograph to the elder statesman of Cassidian vinegrowers:

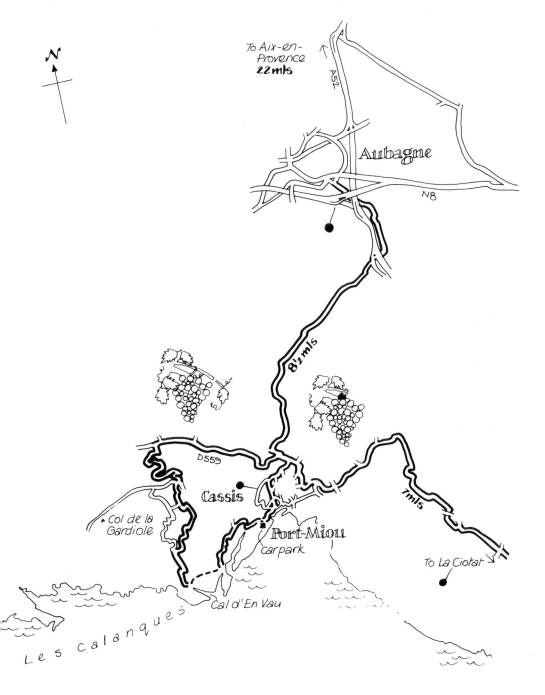

N

To Aix-en-Provence
22 mls

A 52

Aubagne

N8

8½ mls

D559

Cassis

7 mls

Col de la Gardiole

Port-Miou
carpark

To La Ciotat

Cal d'En Vau

Les calanques

'Emile Bodin, who in his Mas Calendal proved with his famous wine that poets are not always liars for our wine is so famous that when Marseilles wants to make a gift of wine to the king she sends for it to Cassis.'

A list of cellars that can be visited is given on p. 16-17.

Four miles along the coast, La Ciotat is a dockyard town in a beautiful setting, with a sandy beach and a centre of thalassotheraphy. It was known from antiquity as a colony of Marseilles, then called Citharista. Another six miles following the coast brings us to Bandol.

One passes the little resorts of Les Lecques and St. Cyr, and a halt could be made at the remarkable little perched village of Le Castellet, dominating the vineyards and, in the Middle Ages, a fortress of no little importance. Owned first by the lords of Baux and then by *le Bon Roi* René, there remains of its medieval past the well-preserved fortifications, a twelfth-century church, carefully restored, and a castle whose oldest part dates back to the eleventh century. The past remains, too, in the numerous houses still existing from the seventeenth and eighteenth centuries, while from the top of the village there is a splendid view across the Ste. Baume range.

Many prefer these little fishing ports, each with their beaches, such as Cassis,

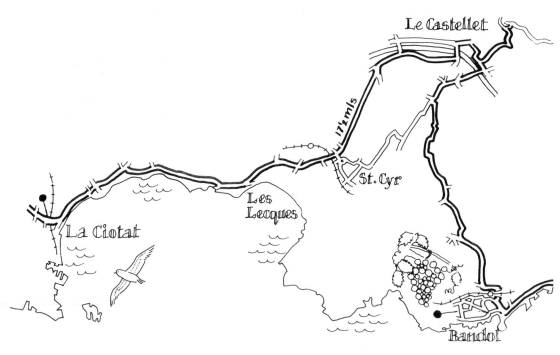

Bandol and Sanary, to those, already more popular on the eastern side of Toulon. Bandol is a particularly favoured resort, its villas shaded by pines and mimosa, with three sandy beaches and protected by wooded hills beyond which stretch the vineyards that produce the most reputed wines of the Côtes de Provence. Over the headland, Sanary is delightful, a little fishing and yachting port, with sandy bays and a palm-lined village protected by wooded hills. It also possesses an eleventh-century Saracen tower. After following this side trip you may prefer to go straight to Toulon (p. 92) or return to Aubagne via the N8.

Aix-en-Provence

Leaving Aubagne we turn north to Aix-en-Provence. Aix is no doubt one of the most beautiful of cities. As far back as the 4th century B.C., the plateau to the north was inhabited by Celts and Ligurians, whose capital was Oppidum d'Entremont. Archeologists excavating there have pronounced it to have been a fairly advanced urban civilisation. These peoples, however, were exposed to trouble from merchants from Marseilles who called on the Roman soldiers to break down their resistance, so that in the year 1 B.C. the consul Sextius took and destroyed Entremont. The following year, in order to protect his conquests, the consul installed a camp which he named Aquae Sextiae (the waters of Sextius), close to the spa which was already known on the site of the present Aix.

Twenty years later the Teutons, marching towards Italy, engaged the Roman army commanded by the General Marius. A trèmendous conflict took place, the Teutons were conquered after days of fierce fighting. The place where the battle was fought was later called the Montagne Ste.-Victoire and many Provençal families took the habit of calling their sons Marius after the general who saved Provence for them.

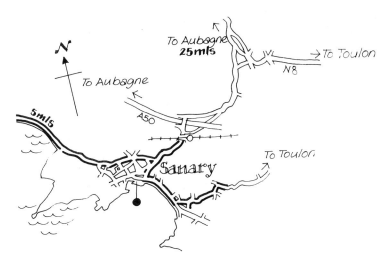

From the twelfth century the counts of Provence made Aix a centre of learning and of the arts. It was also a Bishopric and in 1409 its university was founded. After the reunion of Aix with France in 1486 the governor, representing the king, resided there and the Parliament, created in 1501, assembled there. The city consequently flourished, often being referred to as 'the triumph of the Louis', since from the reign of Louis XIV until Louis XVI its progress continued, so that *le Bon Roi* Réné, count of Provence, could contemplate with pride the aristocratic nature of his city. For Réné was a figure of some importance, with a good knowledge of Greek and Latin, Italian and Hebrew. He also played and composed music, painted and had a knowledge of mathematics, geology and law. Nevertheless, it was not beneath him to work in his vineyards and it was he who introduced the Muscat grape into Provence.

Aix is also closely associated with Mirabeau, who is better known as one of the leaders of the Revolution. His family, however, which during the thirteenth century had emigrated to France from Italy, subsequently obtained the marquisate of Mirabeau in Provence. After a scandalous youth, he married a rich Provençal heiress but, once married, her father cut off her inheritance. Mirabeau's debts were so enormous that finally he was sent into enforced residence at Manosque and from there to the renowned prison of Château d'If. Rejected by the nobles of Provence he suddenly denounced their order as being 'the enemies of the people' and was elected by the Third Estate as deputy for Aix and Marseilles. From the moment he appeared in the Assembly he came to the fore with the fire and thunder of his eloquence. However, he grew to detest the anarchy of the mob and for the remainder of his life he tried to restrain the increasing madness of the Revolution.

Whereas Arles still seems content to dream of her past, Aix, the old capital and most royal of cities, although wrapped in memories, is also a modern spa with a casino and plenty of entertainment. Hardly any town has so successfully managed to blend its historical heritage with youthful activity; in Winter there are the students at the university, in Summer, from mid-July until the beginning of August, people of all ages throng here for the International Festival of Music.

Among the broad, shady avenues the Cours Mirabeau is the main artery, on one side there are cafés and shops (a preponderance of bookshops showing how the intellectual element is still maintained), on the other side, the avenue is bordered by handsome mansions, built in the seventeenth and eighteenth centuries, their sculptured doorways often framed with massive caryatids and wrought-iron balconies. At the end of the Cours the Fontaine du Roi Réné shows the good king holding in his hand a bunch of Muscat grapes.

The cathedral St. Sauveur is in various styles of architecture, dating back in part to the eleventh century. In the immense central nave are two very fine fifteenth-century tryptiques, while the beautiful little baptistry has eight Roman columns supporting a Renaissance dome. The cloister of St. Sauveur is also ravishing, covered by a roof instead of, as is usual, being vaulted. The thirteenth-century church of St. Jean-de-Malte is the chapel of the ancient priory of the Knights of Malta, note the imposing simplicity of the nave.

How much of Aix one is able to see depends, of course, on the time at one's disposal. It was during the seventeenth and eighteenth centuries that the city took on that appearance of sober magnificence which is impressive wherever you look — the seventeenth-century Hotel de Ville and the ancient corn exchange, the Rue Quatre-Septembre with its elegant mansions, the splendid façade of the Hotel d'Arbaud-Jouques and the Tour d'Horloge, and the charming fountain in the Place Alberta. One can almost pick a road or street at random and find that it has its quota of fascinating sculptured doorways and wrought-iron balconies that have weathered the centuries.

It was the birthplace, too, of Cézanne and it was in the surrounding villages that he loved to paint — Gardenne and Bibemus with its cypresses standing like sentinels on the plateau, Tholonet and Estaque, close to the sea where he lived in a fisherman's hut. His studio in Avenue Cézanne remains exactly as it was when he died in 1906 and contains many souvenirs of the artist. Aix has an impressive selection of museums. The Musée Granet, which is the museum of Beaux-Arts and archeology, is housed in the ancient seventeenth-century priory of the Knights of Malta, as well as displaying some of Cézanne's renowned masterpieces there are a number of his lesser-known paintings, sculptures and documents. The French School is well represented, including works of Rigaud and Greuze, David and Ingres. There are works, too, of Rubens, Franz Hals and Rembrandt. The rooms consecrated to archeology have a large number of pieces excavated at nearby Entremont, as well as Roman, Egyptian, Greek, Graeco-Roman and Gallo-Roman sculpture. The Musée des Tapisseries has works from the ancient archbishopric as well as seventeen magnificent seventeenth- and eighteenth-century Beauvais tapestries. Of great interest, too, is the Musée du Vieil Aix, housed in the elegant Hotel d'Estienne St. Jean, which includes souvenirs of the *cortege de la fête-Dieu*, and, above all, a marvellous collection of santons.

These santons are a typical and delightful feature of Provence, until the Revolution they were present in every church. Specialists would make richly clothed figurines which gradually developed into a whole Provençal world in miniature: Tartarin and a peasant woman, the mayor and his wife, a collector of lavender and a fisherman, a shepherd and a gypsy. But it was in the crèche, in the home as in the church, that the imagination was best revealed, with moss-covered stones representing mountains, a mirror for a pond, crumpled silver paper made a waterfall and cottonwool the snow. It is thought that the earliest santons date from around 1764, and they are still made today in the same simple way. They can often be seen in their thousands at the roadside outside the workshop of a *santonnier*. It is probably one of the most typically Provençal souvenirs that one could take away.

Lunch at **Clos de la Violette**, Aix-en-Provence.

Detour

Take the N7 then the D543/943 north from Aix to Bonnieux, then the D36 to join the N100 near Nôtre-Dame de Lumières. This route crosses the magnificent scenery of the hills of Luberon, which are called the Alpes des Lumières, where the sun is said to shine for three hundred and forty days in the year and the air indeed seems to be embalmed with a special purity, perhaps because of its isolation for this is one of the least known regions of Provence.

Our first stop is at Nôtre-Dame de Lumières which became a pilgrimage centre in the seventeenth century when a mysterious light appeared round the chapel of Nôtre-Dame, and, in 1661, an old peasant was mysteriously cured. One visits the sanctuary situated in a delightful park, built between 1663–69. In the crypt the statue of Nôtre-Dame de Lumières stands above the altar.

Four miles further on we pass the Pont Julien, across the Coulon, which owes its name to a colony founded here by Caesar. The three arches of the bridge span the river. Instead of continuing straight on to Apt, it is worth a twenty-mile detour, a splendid drive, overhung by the ochre-coloured cliffs of the Luberon. Roussillon is at the culminating point of the hills which rise up between the Coulon valley and the plateau of the Vaucluse. These hills are constituted of the ochres, the mineral of various shades that is extracted here. Some of these stones are used to adorn the houses, giving an unusually colourful note to the little village. From its Castrum one has a fine view, while half an hour's walk, passing the cemetery, brings one to the cliff edge which looks down over what is called the Chaussée des Géants, an imposing range of deeply cleft rose-red cliffs, dotted with pines and oaks. Five miles from Roussillon, the sleepy old borough of St. Saturnin-d'Apt is dominated by the ruins of her feudal castle and Romanesque chapel surrounded by cypresses. At the top of the village the fifteenth-century Porte Ayguier shows the little that remains of her defence system. Then southwards to Apt, an old Provençal town yet bustling with present day activity, criss-crossed with narrow streets, jostling with shoppers, their baskets loaded with fruit and the other products of the region.

Although Apt was once a Roman colony, her most important monument is the ancient cathedral of St. Anne, the first sanctuary in France to be dedicated to her. It is a composite building, since it was begun in the eleventh century and additions were made until the fourteenth century. The relics, reputed to be those of the Virgin's mother, are preserved in the church. In 1660 Anne of Austria made a pilgrimage to the Chapelle Ste. Anne, afterwards called the Chapelle Royale, and each year there is a pilgrimage here on the last Sunday of July. The archeological museum, housed in a fine eighteenth-century mansion, has a number of Gallo-Roman remains and a splendid collection of earthenware jars. Continuing east for twenty-two miles to Manosque, the road runs below what is

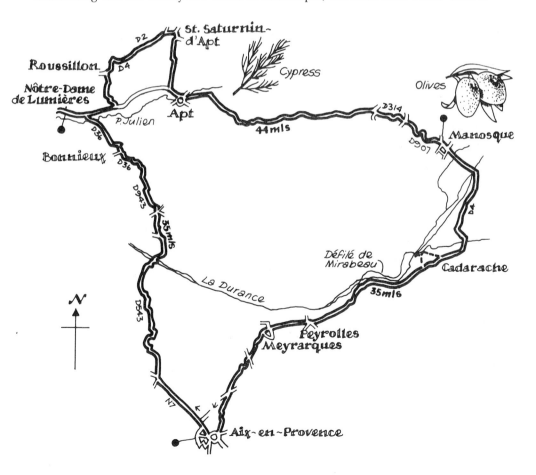

called the Grand Luberon, a wild countryside with magnificent views. Manosque, at the foot of a hill covered with olive groves is close to the Durance, so dear to Giono. He was born here and his *eaux vives* (running water) seems to have a special beauty here, perhaps because of its association with the writer. The town is surrounded by boulevards which have replaced the ancient ramparts although two gateways remain, the fourteenth-century Porte Saunerie, with beautiful machiolated turrets, and the Porte Soubeyran, with an elegant stone railing and a tower decorated with fine wrought-iron work. It is typically Provençal, with narrow streets and high houses, dark beneath the arcades, and through an occasionally open doorway one glances a patio, a garden. The little seventeenth-century Town Hall is in a delightful square, cooled by a fountain. Also seventeenth-century are the Église St. Sauveur and Église Nôtre-Dame-de-Romigier, both fine monuments. Of chief interest, however, is the animated Grand Rue, abounding in ancient houses with balconies, outside staircases and courtyards. At no. 14 Giono spent his childhood, where he became impregnated by the old town, the river and the olive groves he so often described.

Thirty miles separate Manosque from Aix-en-Provence, but it is a route that is full of interest, often following the Durance and crossing the numerous canals that are used for irrigation, supplying water to the towns and for electricity. At Cadarache, a centre for nuclear research, there is also an important dam. The stretch known as the Défilé de Mirabeau is a series of narrow gorges with a bridge across the Durance. A halt could be called at Peyrolles, bordered by her canal, to visit the Église St. Pierre which is part Romanesque, the little Chapelle St. Sepulcre, built in the form of a Greek cross, and an immense seventeenth-century castle which now houses the Town Hall. Meyrarques, too, has an imposing castle which dominates the village.

Detour II

A shorter trip which could be made before leaving Aix would be to make the round of the Montagne Ste.-Victoire. Witness of the great victory at the time of the Romans (see p. 81), in later years the mountain was immortalised by Cézanne who painted it time and again. From earliest times it seems, like Olympus, to have been the object of a veritable cult, worshipped as the temple, high altar and spirit of the region. Seen under different conditions, at dawn, at sunset, in times of storm or mist, one can understand how her contrasts were the inspiration of Cézanne. To those who lived close she seems to have appeared as an invincible soul, exalted and reassuring. Those with the strength can leave the car at the Ferme des Cabassoir and make the long climb up the Chemin des Venturiers. At an altitude of 90m. one reaches the priory of Nôtre-Dame de Ste. Victoire, erected in 1556, from whose terrace there is a fine view, but an even better one rewards those who make the further short climb to the Croix de Provence, a cross 17m. high. Here the panorama embraces the mountains of Provence in all directions with the valley of the Durance below. If one does not make this ascent, the first stop will be to admire the seventeenth-century castle of Vauvenargues. Set on a rocky promontory, it is not open to visitors and was for many years the home of Pablo Picasso who is buried beneath a tree in the park.

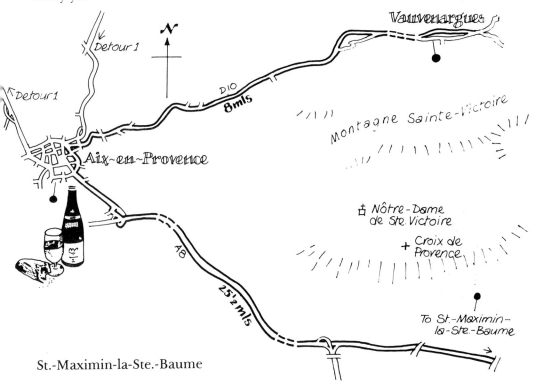

St.-Maximin-la-Ste.-Baume

From Aix one now takes the motorway to St.-Maximin-la-Ste.-Baume. The great mountain range of the Ste. Baume is the highest and most important chain of Provence, one of the great high places of the country. The name of Ste. Baume applies equally to the mountain range, the immense forest which was held sacred by the Romans, and the grotto where tradition relates Mary Magdalene retired to do penitence after having preached the gospel with St. Maximin (who had landed with her at the Stes.-Maries-de-la-Mer) and who became the first bishop of Aix. Again according to legend, she spent thirty-three years in the grotto in prayer and contemplation until, feeling her end near, she went down to the plain and was given the Last Sacrament by St. Maximin. The basilica was built to serve as a shrine for her relics and for those of St. Maximin.

During the first centuries the grotto was greatly venerated and received many pilgrimages until the eleventh century when the rumour was spread that the sacred relics had been stolen and taken to Vezelay in the Yonne, where the great basilica of Ste. Marie Madeleine was built, to become, in the Middle Ages, one of the greatest pilgrimage centres in Europe, being on the route to Compostella. In 1279, however, Charles of Anjou discovered that the relics had never left St. Maximin, after which pilgrims continued to visit both basilicas. Numerous kings of France, the Popes from Avignon, lords and believers from all over the country came to the Ste.-Baume, making it one of the most important pilgrimage centres in the country. For the fête of Sainte Marie-Madeleine (or Mary Magdalene) on July 22nd, a midnight mass is held at the grotto, when the meadows around form a carpet of wild flowers.

The basilica was built by Dominican monks, work began in 1295 and ended in the middle of the sixteenth century, the result is the largest Gothic monument in the south-east of France. The exterior has something of a squat appearance owing to the absence of a spire. Inside, the splendidly sober nave is 235 ft long and 95 ft high, the keystones of the arches bear the coats of arms of the Counts of Provence. The imposing organ was installed in 1773. The choir has a splendid reredos, 94 seventeenth-century choir stalls and an eighteenth-century pulpit, a remarkable display of carved woodwork. In the crypt are the tombs attributed to the saints. The beautiful cloister of the ancient *couvent Royal* has a pleasant garden whose trees give welcome shade when concerts are held there during July. It can be visited throughout the summer months. One leaves the Ste.-Baume with almost the sense of a pilgrim, so closely is the city's history bound to the beginnings of Christianity in France.

Take the autoroute east from Ste.-Baume to Brignoles.

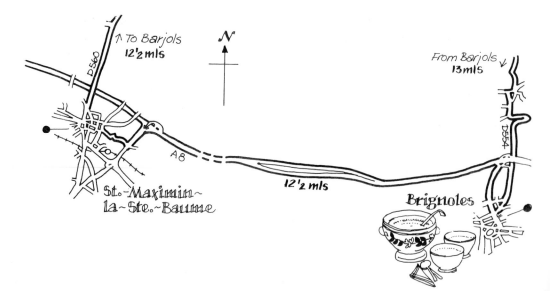

↑ To Barjols
12½ mls

N

From Barjols ↓
13 mls

D560

D554

A8

12½ mls

St.-Maximin-
la-Ste.-Baume

Brignoles

Detour

A detour well worth making, is the fifteen miles north to Barjols, an old borough which, even in high season, has a quality of freshness, partly induced by its twenty fountains. The most important fountain, close to the Town Hall beneath the shade of a great plane tree, is believed to be the largest in Provence. At the end of the village the ancient Hotel de Ponteves has a fine Renaissance doorway while the church, originally Romanesque and restored in the sixteenth century, has a splendid Gothic nave with a beautiful twelfth-century font and a choir with marvellous carvings.

Barjols is known throughout Provence for its Fête des Tripettes, which takes place every four years, the next being in 1989. It is a double procession, being both in honour of St. Marcel to celebrate the return of the saint's relics, which had hitherto been held in a neighbouring monastery; and also to commemorate the occasion when, during a famine, an ox was received down miraculously from heaven. An ox, after being blessed on the steps of the church, is led through the streets accompanied by butchers, cooks and all the participants. After being killed, there are songs and dancing. The following day the ox is roasted on the spit, while the *Dance des Tripettes* is executed, everyone holding their stomachs (hence the name of the dance), accompanied by trumpets, drums and fireworks. The ceremony of the ox dates back to time immemorial, as is the case with much religious folklore, the changing of religion modifies few of these practices. If some consider such popular customs as undermining the spiritual purity, others hold that without it Christianity would be no more than an abstract theology, just as the Sacraments, instituted by Christ, were expressed in symbolism. From Barjols one can take the D554 to Brignoles.

Brignoles

Brignoles is another typically Provençal old town whose narrow streets wind up to the ruins of its castle, owned by the counts of Provence. Its church has a fine Gothic doorway surrounded by Ionian columns and Provençal interior. Brignoles was famed for its prunes until the sixteenth century, and then, since all the plum trees belonged to the lords of the region, during the troubles of the Ligue the people of Brignoles took their revenge by destroying all the eighty thousand trees. Since then, the 'prunes de Brignoles' have come, in fact, from Digne.

Dinner and overnight at **La Paris**, Brignoles.

Clos de la Violette
10 Avenue Violette
Aix-en-Provence
Tel: (42) 23 30 71

This is a very pleasant restaurant with a Michelin star. Its specialities include *Aumonières de poisson aux fleurs de courgette* and *Crepinette d'agneau à la creme d'ail.* To accompany these are the wines of Côteaux d'Aix.

Credit cards: Visa

Le Paris
28 Avenue Dréo
Brignoles
Tel: (94) 69 01 00

This is an unpretentious but pleasant small hotel.

Closed:	15 November to 20th March
Rooms:	16
Facilities:	Restaurant, car park
Food:	Good, plain cooking
Credit cards:	Visa
Rating:	★★

MAS LA CASCADE
Brignoles
Tel: (94) 69 07 85

Situated a mile outside town this is a good average hotel, quiet and comfortably furnished.

Rooms:	10
Facilities:	Garden, conference hall, car park
Rating:	★★

DAY 6

Brignoles to Hyères: approx. 55 miles.

Leaving Brignoles on the D554 as far as Puget-Ville, one joins the N97 for Toulon, a bustling, thriving port, and well worth a visit. Then, eleven miles along the N98 we reach Hyères, the most southerly and oldest resort of the Côte d'Azur, and from where there are excursions to the delightful isles of Porquerolles, Port-Cros and the Ile du Levant.

Back in Hyères, there is plenty to visit in the old town.

Travels in Provence

Breakfast at Brignoles.

Toulon

Leaving Brignoles on the D554 as far as Puget-Ville, one joins the N97 for Toulon, the greatest naval port in France, surrounded by hills crowned with forts. Apart from its association with Napoleon, already mentioned, two points of interest are that in the *vieille Darse* or wet harbour, one can see the upper level of a seventeenth-century galley. The other point is that in Roman times Toulon was famed for its *pourpre*, a colour that for long was reserved only for emperors' use. On the coast here were numerous cockles, which, when crushed, released a substance that was subsequently treated until it produced the purple with which wool and silk were dyed. During excavations in its arsenal the foundation of one of these dyers was discovered.

Even if one is not interested in visiting the Musée marine, one can wander through the narrow streets of the old town, always animated, always seeming to jostle with sailors home on leave. A number of its houses date back to the eighteenth century, while the cathedral was begun in the eleventh century and restored at different periods. Its massive spire was built in 1740; its interior is Gothic. The most attractive of its squares is the Place Puget with a great sculptured fountain.

The best possible view over the magnificent roadstead is to leave Toulon on the D559 and continue round by La Seyne and Tamaris to the peninsula of St. Mandrier.

Ile de Porquerolles

Eleven miles along the N98 brings us to Hyères port, from where one embarks for the Iles d'Or or Golden Isles as those of Porquerolles, Port-Cros and the Ile du Levant are called.

The boat trip to the Porquerolles takes thirty minutes from the port of Hyères, fifteen if made from the peninsula of Giens.

In the past the coastline of Porquerolles was inhabited by the Romans who called it Prote (meaning 'the first'), while Port-Cros they called Mese (the

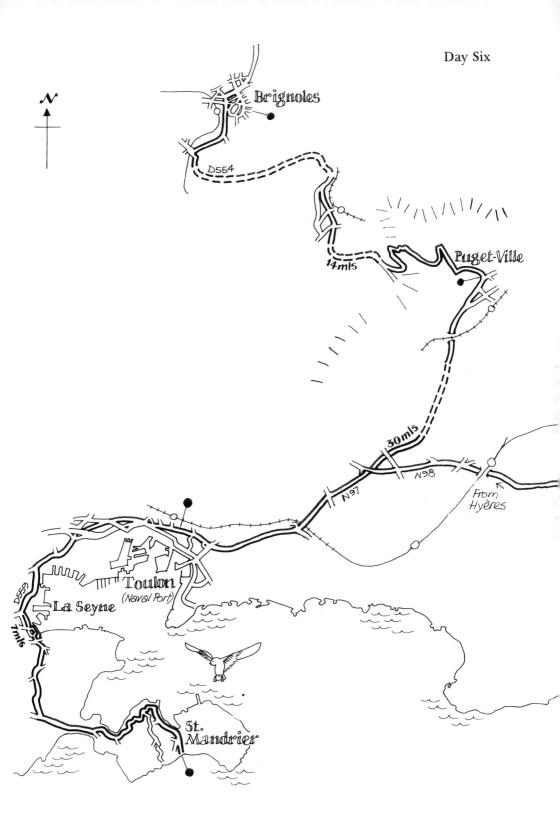

N

Brignoles

D554

14 mls

Puget-Ville

From Hyères

30 mls

N97

N98

Toulon
(Naval Port)

La Seyne

D559

7 mls

St.
Mandrier

middle) since it is situated between the other two islands.

The little harbour of Porquerolles is now filled with luxury yachts and surrounded by red houses, unfortunately not in the local style. However, the village has changed little since it was built in the nineteenth century by Army administration and it evokes more an African village than Provençal. It has, nonetheless, an undisputed charm, with a little church, a few fishermen's houses and eucalyptus trees of different varieties. The isle, however, is Provençal indeed in its luxuriant fertility, with olive groves and vineyards, orchards and pinewoods, figs and a strange, rough barked tree called the bellombra which was imported from Mexico. A popular way of visiting the island is to hire a bicycle.

Port-Cros

Port-Cros is in striking contrast to Porquerolles, hilly and with a marvellously rich vegetation, maquis scattered with rosemary and wild asparagus and wild boar roaming unmolested. The whole island is a National Park so the flora and fauna are strongly protected. There is even a little animal unknown anywhere else in Provence, the Discoglasse sarde, a kind of green frog with a mark like a C on its back which is found in the Greek islands and Sardinia.

Perhaps it is because one really has the feeling here that man has been chased out by nature that it has always been especially popular with writers. Simenon situated one of his novels here, as did E.M. de Vogüe. St. John Perse looked across to it from his villa at Giens and it was due to André Malraux that it became a National Park.

Lunch at **Hotel le Manoir**, Port-Cros.

Ile du Levant

Lastly, the Ile du Levant is less frequented since it is occupied largely by the French navy, in summer by a nudist colony. It is closest to Le Lavandou, thirty-five minutes by boat.

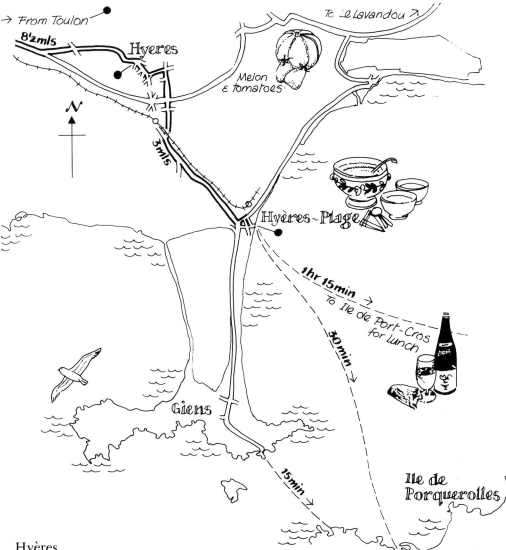

Hyères

There is plenty of interest in Hyères, reputed to have one of the mildest climates in France. It is certainly the oldest resort, Catherine de Medici used to come here in the winter. A century later it also became popular with the English who appreciated walking in the forests of the beautiful Maures Hills with which it is flanked.

But to go back to its beginnings. Excavations close to the sea, in the district that is now called Almanarre, have disclosed the remains of a Greek colony,

95

Olbia, followed by the Roman town of Pomponiana. In the Middle Ages, however, the inhabitants left the coast in favour of the hill where the lords of Fos built their castle. It was later taken by the Counts of Provence who rebuilt it in the thirteenth century. Important ruins still remain, notably the crenellated towers of its keep.

Like so many of these towns, Hyères consists of the old town, which slopes down from the castle, and below stretches the modern part with palatial hotels, good shops and wide avenues lined by palms and oleanders. It has a beach flanked by umbrella pines. In the old Hyères the Porte Masaillon leads into a street which used to be the *Grand Rue*, where Renaissance doorways are numerous. At the end, the Place Masaillon hums with activity during its daily market. Its fourteenth-century tower of St. Blaise is all that remains of the ancient seat of the Order of Templars.

The monumental steps and doorway of the Renaissance church of St. Paul are very imposing, and on entering one should not miss the delightful crèche of Provençal santons in the decor of a medieval village.

Dinner and overnight at **Pins d'Argent**, Hyères-Plage.

Hotel le Manoir
Ile de Port-Cros
Tel: (94) 05 90 52

At the entrance to the marvellously named Vallon de la Solitude, the hotel is housed in a little castle that was built in 1760, surrounded by eucalyptus, and open from the beginning of May until October.

Pins d'Argent
Hyères-Plage
Tel: (94) 57 63 60

A good average and quiet hotel set in a park.

Closed:	Wednesdays, except in July and August
Rooms:	20
Facilities:	Restaurant, swimming pool, car park
Credit cards:	American Express, Visa
Food:	A good value menu
Rating:	★★

REINE JANE
Aygaude-Ceinturon
Tel: (94) 66 32 64

Two miles from Hyères, this small comfortable hotel is close to the port.

Closed:	1st December to 15th January
Rooms:	15
Facilities:	Restaurant, pleasant terrace
Credit cards:	Eurocard, Visa
Food:	Menus are reasonably priced.
Rating:	★★

HYÈRES: USEFUL INFORMATION

Tourist Office:	Av. Belgique
	Tel: (94) 65 18 55
Population:	41739
Altitude:	40 metres
Facilities:	Airport, golf course, camp sites, including the 3 star Domaine du Ceinturon, water sports

Bormes-les-Mimosas

DAY 7

From Hyères to St. Tropez: approx. 40 miles.

Leaving Hyères on the N98 we can look across to the Summer residence of the President of the Republic, the fort of Brégançon, jutting out to sea on its peninsula. Soon after Bormes-les-Mimosas, a detour can be made into the Maures Hills. Otherwise we continue along the coast by Le Lavandou and Cavalaire, after which the road winds up to la Croix Valmer and Gassin.

Leaving Gassin we dip down into St. Tropez where plenty will be found to occupy the afternoon.

Travels in Provence

Breakfast at Hyères.

Leaving Hyères on the N98 look across to the Summer residence of the President of the Republic, Brégançon fort, jutting out to sea on its peninsula.

Bormes-les-Mimosas

Bormes-les-Mimosas, fourteen miles from Hyères, is an old Provençal town flanked by the Maures Hills. Its labyrinth of streets are mellow with age, semi-Moorish. The Église St. Trophyme, close to the Hotel de Ville, was built in the eighteenth century and has three naves. There is an inspiring Chemin de Croix and some fine paintings. The old streets lead up to the partially-restored castle of the lords of Fos, from where there is one of the most splendid views over the Iles d'Hyères.

Detour

Those with the time can make a rewarding detour into the forest of Dom in the massif of the Maures, by turning inland at Bormes to the picturesque little village of Collobrières, with an old bridge beneath which the water flows swiftly past. *Marrons glacés*, are made here and also chestnut jam. Soon after Collobrières one should take the road which branches off to the right as far as the Chartreuse de la Verne, just fifteen miles from Bormes. This dramatically beautiful spot is where the ruins of the old monastery stand close to a spring. The Chartreuse was founded in 1176 and restored several times until the Revolution, when the monks deserted it. The bluish tint of some of its stones, hewn out of the rock, give a strange character to the remaining walls.

Retracing our steps almost to Collobrières, we take the road north to Nôtre-Dame des Anges which, at 780m. is the highest point in the range. Like that of the Chartreuse the site is admirable, set among jagged rocks. A hermitage stands close to the summit, a Merovingian foundation which venerated Nôtre-Dame and

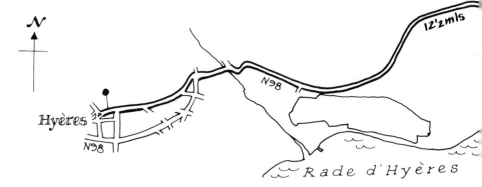

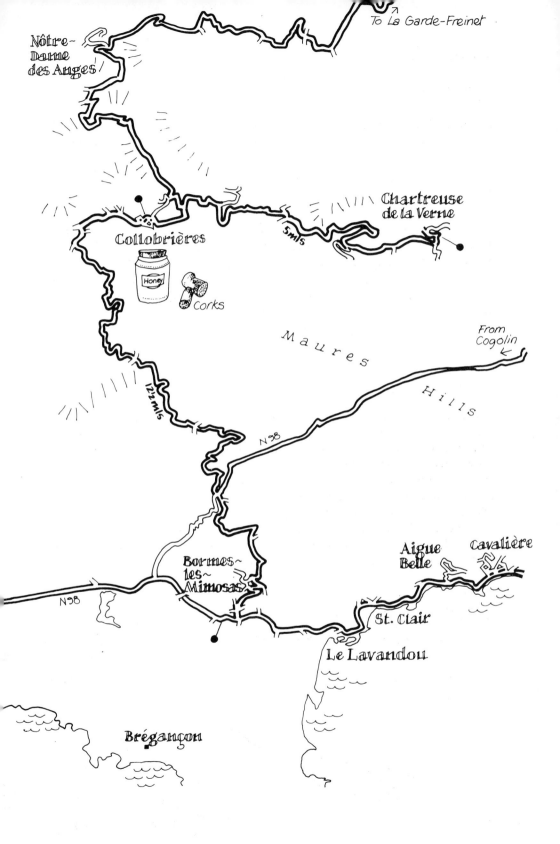

which is still the scene of pilgrimages. The building was reconstructed in the nineteenth century with the purpose of sheltering visitors and pilgrims.

The road continues on to La Garde-Freinet, one of many Moorish strongholds in this region, and which they held for a century, it being a position of great strategic importance. The ruins of its castle mingle with the rocks which surround it, but the village has maintained all its local crafts, including honey production and the making of corks and *marrons glacées* called the *marrons du Luc*.

Then comes Grimaud, one of the oldest communes of Provence, during the time of the Greek occupation it was called Athenopolis. And so it remained until the Revolution when the Squire Grimaldus renamed it after his family. Jean Grimaldi acquired the castle from the Count of Provence as a reward for services rendered, for he played an important part in driving off the Saracen invaders. The streets of the little village have retained all their medieval character, the Rue des Templiers shaded by arcades.

The next village is Cogolin which, like La Garde-Freinet, has retained all her traditional character as well as being a hive of local industry. One of the chief occupations of the inhabitants is making rugs and furnishing fabrics. The workshops, in the Avenue G. Clemenceau, can be visited. In Cogolin they also make pipes from the roots of the heather that covers the Maures Hills, and corks, again from the Maures which are rich in cork pines. Viticulture holds an important place in the local economy as well. The Maures Hills flank the coast between Hyères and St. Raphael. They are a range complete in themselves and one of the oldest, comparative with the Auvergne, although nowhere higher than 780 m. and without a trace of that limestone which is such a common feature of Provence. Cloaked with cork-oaks, chestnuts and umbrella pines, they make marvellous walking country. Whatever path one takes the undergrowth is thick, dotted with boulders, with patches of heather and fallen trees, often unfortunately, ravaged by forest fires. Return to Bormes along the N98 or go straight to St. Tropez.

Le Lavandou

From Bormes we should go down to the bay, which has a yacht harbour and three sandy beaches close to those of Le Lavandou, a delightful little fishing village. Although flower lovers might like to think that its name was derived from 'lavender', it is more likely that it was from the *lavandiers* or washerwomen who used to work beside the little river of the Bataillier. Continuing along this eight mile stretch of road known as the Corniche de Maures, one passes the quiet resorts of St. Clair and Aigue Belle, Cavalière and Pramousquier, all with sheltered sandy beaches. Probably the most sheltered of all is Rayol-Canadel, at the foot of the chain of the Pradels and flanked by pinewoods. From the village a monumental staircase, cascading with flowers, leads down to the beach with, half way down, gardens and a terrace. After which Cavalaire-sur-Mer, with three miles of wide, sandy beaches and flanked by forests, is particularly popular for family holidays.

La Croix Valmer

From Cavalaire the road winds up to la Croix Valmer, a little village whose vineyards produce the Côtes de Provence.

A stone cross commemorates an event of the very distant past, for it is related that when the Roman Emperor, Constantin, came from Italy to conquer this region, he saw, on this spot, the appearance above him of a cross bearing the words: *in hoc signo Vinces* — by this sign you will conquer. It not only announced, indeed, his next conquest but also that of Christianity. From the time that he was first proclaimed Augustus, Constantin ignored the edicts issued against the Christians, and thus allowed the new religion to spread quickly throughout western Europe. At a time when the Roman Empire was divided between two brothers-in-law, Licinius and Constantin, a difference of policy soon showed itself. In the final struggle Licinius made himself the champion of the old paganism, Constantin of the new religion. Almost the first solemn act of his monarchy was to make the Christian religion the religion of the State.

Gassin

The next village, Gassin, Moorish in appearance, has a little church with a modern Chemin de Croix accompanied by a commentary of the artist.

Lunch at **Auberge la Verdoyante**, Gassin.

After lunch, continue on to Ramatuelle which is one of the most delightful of these hill villages. Surrounded by vineyards and gay with flowers, the narrow, often vaulted streets huddle round the little sixteenth-century church, in whose cemetery lies the film star, Gerard Philipe.

Like Gassin, there is a Moorish aspect about the village, and one must remember that between the eighth and eighteenth centuries this part of the coast was menaced by frequent raids of pirates from North Africa. The people of Provence usually refer to them as Saracens, a term by which they denote indifferently Arabs, Moors, Turks and Barbarians.

St. Tropez

One dips down into St. Tropez, eleven miles from Cavalaire. St. Trope, as it is popularly called, has for the last two decades become almost synonymous with film stars and the variety world which made it so fashionable. In the Summer it draws hordes of tourists who are well catered for with night clubs. restaurants and every kind of entertainment.

This, happily, is the entirely artificial side, it was the very beauty of its situation which originally made it popular during the nineteenth century with such celebrated figures as Maupassant and Colette, Matisse and Marcel Pagnol. For those who consider it only as the playground of topless beauties, the fact remains that there is probably no longer a resort along the Mediterranean coast without topless bathing. St. Tropez is not to be condemned alone. In any case there are numerous small coves and rock-bound bays along this coast enough to satisfy the most traditionally minded.

The first settlers in the little port of St. Tropez were the Greeks, in 470 B.C. Its name, however, is derived from the legend of a centurian Christian, by the name of Torpes, who was beheaded on the order of the Emperor Nero. His lifeless body was put into a boat together with a cock and a dog and pushed out to sea. When the boat landed his body was intact, neither of the animals had touched it. The place where it came ashore was called St. Tropez. The

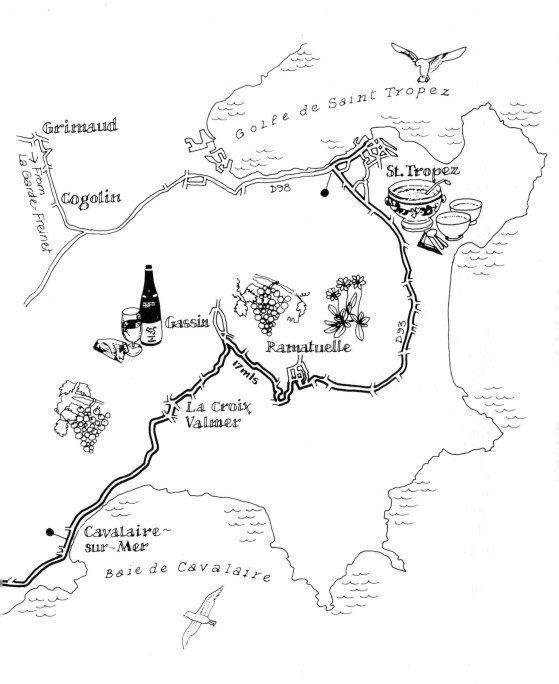

saint is commemorated on the occasion of one of the two *bravades* that take place annually, a *bravade* being an organisation in charge of celebrations. The religious celebration began in the fifteenth century. Since then, on the 16th and 17th of May a gilt bust of the saint is carried through the town followed by the captain elected by the municipal council and members of the *bravade*. The picturesque procession is accompanied by a large crowd. The second *bravade* is associated with local history and takes place on June 15th, the date on which, in the year 1637, twenty-two Spanish galleys attempted to capture the town and were driven off thanks to the gallant defenders of St. Tropez.

The harbour, which saw the beginnings of St. Tropez, is now the very hub of fashionable life, the hitherto little fishing village is afloat with yachts of every description, the rose and ochre walls of its old houses transformed into cafés and cabarets, antique shops and every sort of establishment that spells luxury. The bronze statue of Pierre André Suffren de St. Tropez surveys this cosmopolitan scene and the town is proud of its hero who fought gallantly in America, giving the English a bad time in India at the end of his campaign which included the Cape of Good Hope, the Ile of the Reunion and Sumatra after which he was named Vice-Admiral. His family were lords of St. Tropez.

At the other end of the port the Musée d'Annonciade has a rich collection of modern art, for among the numerous artists who frequented St. Tropez were Matisse and Bonnard. The little fishing port with the old tower is one of the corners they best loved to paint. Only a few steps away one passes beneath an ancient gateway into the old town, active too, but still Provençal. The nineteenth-century church is baroque in style, with some finely carved woodwork and the bust of St. Tropez.

Of older date is the citadelle with a fine keep, reinforced by three round towers in the sixteenth century. From the fort of the ramparts one has a splendid view over the gulf of St. Tropez and across to the Maures Hills. The Musée de la Marine is housed in the keep and its exhibition is an excellent way to learn the town's history.

Dinner and overnight at **La Mandarine**, St. Tropez.

Auberge la Verdoyante
Gassin
Tel: (94) 56 16 23

A delightful small inn. The local wine is to be recommended.

La Mandarine
Route de Tahiti
St. Tropez
Tel: (94) 97 21 00

This is a comfortable, quiet hotel.

Closed:	15th October until Easter
Rooms:	40
Facilities:	Swimming pool, restaurant, car park
Credit cards:	American Express, Diner's Club, Visa
Food:	A la Carte
Rating:	★★★

LEVANT
Route des Salins
St. Tropez
Tel: (94) 97 33 33

This very comfortable hotel has a pleasant garden and terrace.

Closed:	12th October to 22nd March
Rooms:	28
Facilities:	Restaurant, swimming pool, car park
Credit cards:	American Express, Diner's Club, Visa
Food:	Specialises in grills
Rating:	★★

St. TROPEZ: USEFUL INFORMATION

Tourist Office: Quai Jean-Jaures
Tel: (94) 97 45 21
Population: 6248

107

Fréjus — the cathedral cloisters

DAY 8

St. Tropez to Valescure (St. Raphael): approx. 27 miles.

Situated in the heart of the bay, four miles from St. Tropez, Port Grimaud is one of the most visited spots on this coast, a Provençal village encircled by the sea.

Leaving it on the N98 brings us to St. Maxime, facing St. Tropez across the bay. After a visit, we continue on, past the pleasant little resorts of Les Issambres and St. Aygulf, with a halt here for lunch.

St. Aygulf adjoins St. Raphael, one of the most animated resorts on this coast. It has plenty of interest too, although its past cannot compare with its prodigious neighbour, Fréjus, which demands as much time as can be devoted to it.

Travels in Provence

Breakfast at St. Tropez.

Port Grimaud

Situated in the heart of the bay, four miles from St. Tropez, Port Grimaud is one of the most visited spots on this coast, a Provençal village encircled by the sea. As soon as one steps across the bridge one comes under the spell of this little port which literally rose out of the sands in 1966 when it was built, in the regional style of fishermen's houses — ochre walls, red tiles and brown, green or blue shutters — crossed by a network of canals.

It is sometimes called 'the modern Venice', although very much a Venice in miniature. Like Venice it is inaccessible to cars, except those of the residents and delivery vans. There is a vast car park outside for visitors, who come all the year round. For if, during the winter, the rhythm of life here slows down, unlike other tourist centres the shops and restaurants are under contract to remain open for nine months of the year. In any case, most of the residents are yacht-lovers and here they have found something near to the sailor's Paradise, they need wind but not necessarily sunshine.

Wander along the alleys — the Rue des Deux-Ports, Rue des Artisans and Rue de l'Ile Longue; push open the door of the ecumenical church, dedicated to St. Francis of Assisi. Then take a boat round the labyrinth of canals from which one can appreciate the imaginative planning: the fronts of the houses bordering shrub-lined streets, the backs abutting a canal, where each has a berthing right alongside, the groups of houses separated by canals and reached by bridges.

One can sit on a café terrace, watching the activity in the colourful market, and contemplate on how one man's dream created all this. Francis Spierry was a little boy of six living in Zurich, when he first became fascinated by the model of a lacustine city displayed in the museum there. Many years later, although trained as an architect, his passion for the sea remained. Thus was born the project which, at the time, was regarded with the greatest mistrust by his associates and indeed is still the subject of controversy. In 1962, sailing close to St. Tropez, he noticed the marshes of what was to become Port Grimaud. It took him four years to obtain the necessary authorisation and to overcome all the obstacles that seemed to bar the achievement.

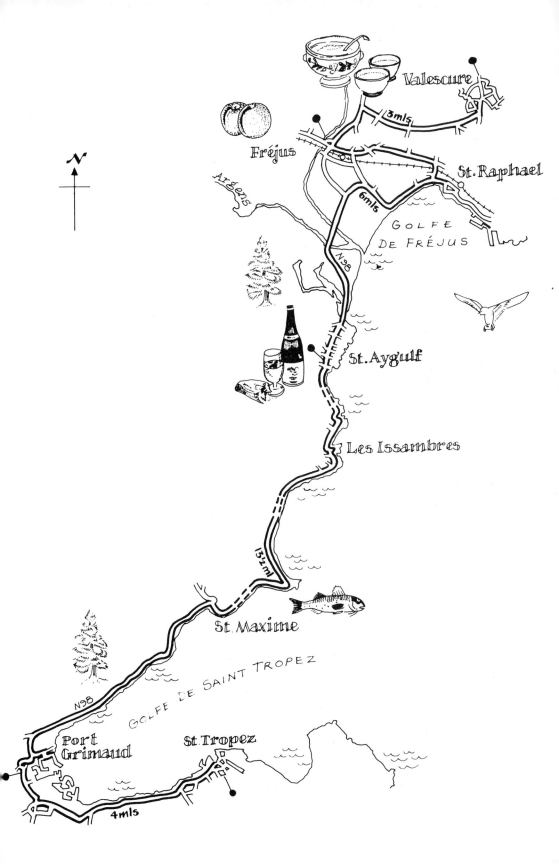

N

Valescure

3mls

Fréjus

St. Raphael

6mls

GOLFE
DE FRÉJUS

Argens

N98

St. Aygulf

Les Issambres

13½ml

St. Maxime

GOLFE DE SAINT TROPEZ

N98

Port
Grimaud

St. Tropez

4mls

Ste. Maxime

Leaving Port Grimaud on the N98 brings us to Ste. Maxime, facing St. Tropez across the bay. Ste. Maxime's harbour is thought to have been the Roman Sinus Sambracitanus. Today it is a flourishing resort with a fishing and yacht harbour, a sandy beach and pinewoods sloping up to the Maures. It is a pleasant little town, Place Victor Hugo at the centre, shaded by magnificent plane trees. Close to the church, which has a fine interior, is the Tour Carrée des Dames, a tower originally erected by the monks of the Lérins for defence purposes.

Issambres

From Ste. Maxime we continue on to the little resort of Issambres, certainly less controversial than Port Grimaud from which it is ten miles distant. Issambres is ideal for a family holiday, there is no casino, no night clubs worth mentioning, but there are two good beaches, rocks and wonderful walks in the hills behind, for it lies between the ranges of the Maures and the Esterel.

Lunch at **La Glycine**, St. Aygulf.

Issambres is separated from St. Raphael by the pleasant little resort of St. Aygulf, where we halt for lunch. It has a sandy, rock-bound beach set among pinewoods, facing the bay of Fréjus and the mass of the Esterel.

St. Raphael

St. Raphael is one of the most popular and animated resorts west of the Esterel, by which its beaches are protected. It has everything in the way of entertainment including a casino and a harbour that is one of the best known on the coast for pleasurecraft — with berths for up to a thousand and eight hundred yachts. One of its claims to fame is that it was from here on April 28th, 1814, that Napoleon embarked for exile in Elba, to land at Golfe Juan for the Hundred Days in the following year.

St. Raphael's twelfth-century church, built in Roman Provençal style, used to serve as a fortress where the inhabitants took refuge during invasions from the pirates who constantly ravaged this coast.

Although its past cannot compare with that of its prodigious neighbour, Fréjus, they are similar in that St. Raphael was a Roman settlement where rich citizens built themselves magnificent villas until, in the tenth century, it was sacked by Saracens. It did not gain status as a shipping centre until the Middle Ages, after the hitherto important naval base of Fréjus had become silted up.

Fréjus

Fréjus was founded in the year 49 B.C. by Julius Caesar himself who gave his creation the name of Forum Juli, of which the modern name is a corruption. It was here that the Aurelian Way turned inland, making Fréjus at once a great commercial centre and an important strategic point on the way through to Spain. Ten years later the Emperor Augustus created the great naval base, constructing two hundred light, swift galleys which won him the battle of Actium in 31 B.C. against the heavier vessels of Anthony and Cleopatra.

After this the development of the town was rapid, calculated to have reached as many as forty thousand inhabitants, many more than at present. The sea has receded so far that it is difficult to realise how great a port this used to be. The Lanterne d'Auguste, although so named, is thought to have been built at a later date to guide fishermen back to harbour.

Although Fréjus was primarily a naval port, excavations show that it altered little from other Roman cities. These Roman remains, though mutilated, are extensive. Only one tower is left of the gateway in the fortifications and the once great viaduct is no more than a series of ruined pillars. The amphitheatre, however, is considered the oldest still existing in France. Unlike the other great Roman amphitheatres, built for a wealthy public, that of Fréjus is essentially simple in style, the spectators were mostly the military, who probably built it themselves and in some haste as well. Four corridas are held here during the summer months.

The theatre, of which a fair number of the ruined tiers remain, was built at the same period. There are also traces of the citadelle where the praetorium was held, and a fine arcade known as the Porte d'Orée.

The medieval episcopal city is well preserved and extremely interesting, grouped around its cathedral which resembles more a fortress than a church.

113

It was, in fact, intended as a fortified sanctuary when it was built in the tenth century on the site of an ancient basilica which, in turn, was founded over a primitive temple dedicated to Jupiter. The magnificent Renaissance doorway is protected by woodwork. In the interior the nave is heavily vaulted, held up by great stone pillars. The fifteenth-century choir stalls are finely carved and the handsome reredos dedicated to St. Marguerite. On the dome of the spire, which was added two centuries later, is a crenellated tower intended to protect the episcopal palace, erected in the fourteenth century in the rose-coloured stone of the Esterel.

Separated from the cathedral by an imposing wrought-iron porch, the baptistry, built in the fourth or fifth century, is one of the earliest examples in France of early Christian art. It is a little square building, the walls of the interior are lined with small alcoves, separated by black granite columns, the whole is covered by a cupola which was added in the nineteenth century, supported by columns. Excavations have discovered the original flooring of white marble and the mosaics that decorated the alcoves.

The doors at each end had originally separate uses, by one those to be baptised entered, for they were usually adult, by the other, the triumphal archway, the newly-baptised Christians left. A staircase leads up to the ravishing cloister, built between the twelfth and thirteenth centuries. The Gothic arches of the gallery are supported by slender pillars, roofed with red pantiles. In the centre of the little garden an old well is guarded by cypresses.

Dinner and overnight at **Golf Hotel de Valescure**, St. Raphael.

La Glycine
St. Aygulf
Tel: (94) 81 30 23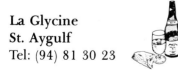

We thought this a pleasant little restaurant with a menu of very good value. We accompanied our meal with an excellent Côtes de Provence.

Golf Hotel de Valescure
St. Raphael
(D37 and Route Golf)
Tel: (94) 52 01 57

Situated between Fréjus and St. Raphael, this really marvellous hotel, with views over its beautiful golf course, seems a haven of tranquillity.

Closed:	September 15th to December 20th and January 7th to March 20th
Rooms:	40
Facilities:	Golf course, swimming pool, tennis courts, car park
Credit cards:	American Express, Diner's Club, Eurocard, Visa
Food:	Well-finished and carefully cooked meals
Wine:	Côtes de Provence
Rating:	★★★

LA POTINIÈRE
Boulouris
St. Raphael
Tel: (94) 95 21 43

This is another quiet, very comfortable hotel set in a park.

Closed:	November 5th to December 20th
Rooms:	21
Facilities:	Swimming pool, tennis courts, restaurant, car park
Credit cards:	American Express, Diner's Club
Food:	Specialities include delicious *Sole souflée aux écrevisses, Escalope de foie gras aux raisins* and *Coeur de Charolais en terrine*
Rating:	★★

St. RAPHAEL: USEFUL INFORMATION

Tourist Office:	Rue W. Rousseau
	Tel: (94) 95 16 87
Population:	24310
Facilities:	Camp sites (4 star and 3 star), golf course, railway station

Cannes

DAY 9

Valescure (St. Raphael) to Menton: approx. 60 miles.

Leaving Valescure on the D37, after four miles, instead of turning south to Agay, those with the time can continue over the Col Belle-Barbe to explore the beautiful hills of the Esterel.

Otherwise, after leaving Valescure, one heads down to Agay for the Esterel coast road. After dipping down into La Napoule, resorts follow one after the other, one of the most celebrated, of course, being the ever-popular Cannes from where one can take a boat across to the Iles de Lérins.

After Cannes, the elegant resort of Juan-les-Pins adjoins Antibes, dominated by her imposing Fort Carrée. Leaving Antibes, the road runs straight along the coast to Nice which one enters by the magnificent Promenade des Anglais, the most celebrated esplanade in the world.

I suggest visiting Nice on the following day to enable us to reach Menton by the upper corniche from where the views are magnificent, and the perched village of Eze not to be missed, returning next day by the coast road where the resorts are situated. The evening can be spent exploring the delightful town of Menton.

The immense popularity of the coastal resorts between Valescure and Menton can lead to appalling traffic jams at certain times of the year. If traffic congestion is causing excessive delays at any part of the trip, you can take the autoroute — A8 — to move more quickly between sections of today's route.

Travels in Provence

Breakfast at Valescure.

Leaving Valescure on the D37.

Detour

After 4 miles, instead of turning south to Agay, travellers not pressed for time can continue over the Col Belle-Barbe to explore the Esterel hills. After the col, the car should be left in the Parking and the path taken — only half an hour's walk there and back — to the appropriately named Ravin du Mal Infernet, for the deep red might well be the fires of Hell. It is one of the many deep ravines of this range where the scenery is grandiose, with boulders and jagged crags. At the end of the path is the little lake of the Ecureil.

All along this winding route, known as the Pic de l'Ours, which takes one over the Col du Mistral and the Col des Suvières, one has splendid views across to the sea and over the Pic de l'Ours, whose summit, at an altitude of no more than 496m. gives nevertheless an impression of much greater height on account of its rugged, barren site. Close to the Col des Trois Termes is another ravishing plateau known as the Aire de Morts, though why so named it would be hard to guess. The stretch between the Col Nôtre-Dame and the Col des Lentisques is probably the most splendid of the whole range, so varied are the views over the coast, where the rocks plunge down to the sea and across to Cap d'Antibes, the gulf of La Napoule and the Iles de Lérins.

Detour II

If you prefer not to follow the coastal route to Cannes there is another road, further north and starting from Fréjus, which formed the old Aurelian Way, the most important of the Roman Empire, that used to link Rome with Genoa, Fréjus and Aix. It takes one up to the foot of Mt. Vinaigre which, at 618m. is the highest summit of the Esterel. For those who would walk up to its top, it is a matter of only half an hour and the view, of course, is splendid.

Two miles further along the road the Auberge des Adrets is the name of an inn frequented by the notorious bandit Gaspard de Bresse and his band, who made their refuge in a nearby grotto. In times past the Esterel was a haunt of brigands and highwaymen

118

who held up travellers along this much frequented route. Gaspard de Bresse, who was something of a Dick Turpin, lived in the eighteenth century and was well known, not only for his exploits but for his elegance and love of ostentation. The distance from Fréjus to Cannes by this route is twenty miles.

Agay

Although the Côte d'Azur, or Riviera, is traditionally the most popular part of the Mediterranean coast it should be remembered that along the forty-mile stretch between La Napoule and Menton it is only between La Napoule and

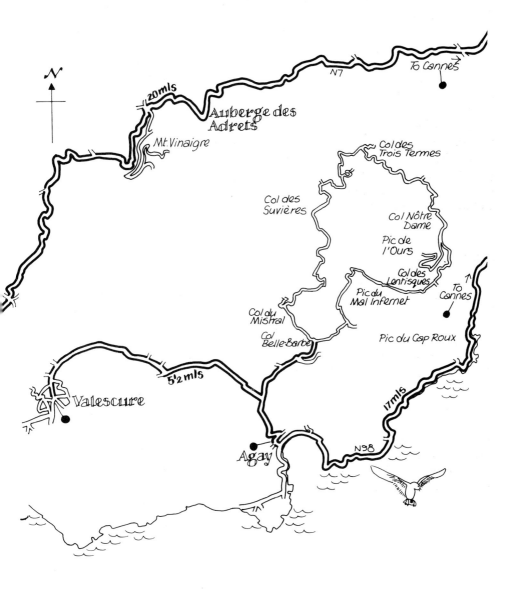

Nice that there are sandy beaches. Nice itself has only a belt of shingle to offer. On the other hand, you can be sure of near perfect weather, protected, as it is, by the Alps which form a barrier against the Mistral. Despite the Mistral, many holiday-makers prefer the resorts further west on account of the sandy beaches and little rock bound bays such as Agay, for which one should head after leaving Valescure.

Nestling deep in its bay, it is an enchanting spot, with a wide sandy beach and, around the corner, a little shady creek. It was already popular in the long distant past when it was the Oètgina of a Ligurian tribe, the Agathon of the Greeks and the Portus Agathonis of the Romans. Excavations have in fact shown vestiges of a Roman chapel dedicated to St. Agatha. Agay also had its more recent history, but nothing was left after the last war due to repeated bombings from American planes, destined for the viaduct of Anthéor. Agay is dominated by the great red rocks overhanging the Esterel coast road. The road is a tremendous feat of engineering, hewn out of the rocks and open since 1903. Paths up into the hills can be taken just as easily from this route as from the inland roads. One is up to the Rocher de St. Barthélemy where a flight of steps hewn out of the rock leads up to the summit. It takes half an hour there and back. Another is up to the Pic du Cap Roux, which is a much longer climb since the summit is at 542m., but the panorama from the orientation table is magnificent.

This Esterel range used to be covered with the same type of forest as the Maures: pines and cork-oaks, but it has been devastated so frequently by forest fires that the vegetation now mostly consists of great stretches of scrub and heathland, scattered with gorse and broom and, in Spring, a carpet of wild flowers.

La Napoule

At the headland known as the Pointe de l'Aiguille one dips down to La Napoule which, until the disastrous frost of 1985, used to be known as the capital of mimosa. Situated at the foot of the hill of San Peyre, which can be easily reached on foot, La Napoule has three sandy beaches and, naturally, a yacht harbour. In the fourteenth century a massive fortress was built here, on the ruins of a Roman victualling yard. It was transformed by the American sculptor Henry Clews and one can now visit both the gardens and the interior as well as the chapel and cloister.

Cannes

Cannes, at a distance of twenty-two miles from St. Raphael, was first made
famous by Lord Brougham. Before that it was a little fishing village of no more
importance than any along this coast, its name of Cannes derives from the
quantity of *cannes*, or reeds and rushes that flourished in the harbour.
In 1834 Lord Brougham had intended spending a holiday in Italy. He arrived
at Nice to find that there was an epidemic of cholera further east so decided
instead to explore the coast in the other direction. Until he came to Cannes.
So delighted was he by this (then) little seaside village that he built himself a
house there where he spent every winter for thirty-four years.

Although everyone seems to know that it was Lord Brougham who first made
Cannes popular, not much seems to be known about the man himself. Henry
Peter Brougham, who was born in Edinburgh, was a conspicuous lawyer and
statesman. In London he attracted special attention by an appearance which

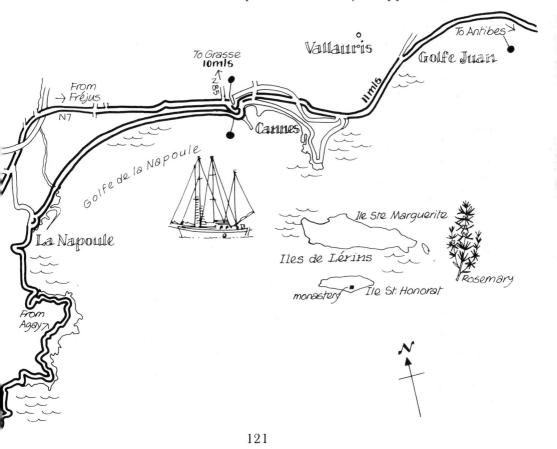

he made at the bar of the House of Commons. He entered Parliament as a Liberal and was a strong opponent of the slave trade. In 1830 he became Chancellor of the new Ministry where his eloquence greatly aided the passing of the Reform Act. On the fall of the Ministry in 1832 he retired from office and never returned to it, although his voice was frequently heard as a fearless advocate of political and social reform.

Evidently the man who settled in Cannes was of considerable importance, otherwise it is unlikely that his example would have been followed, as was the case, by royalty, dukes and millionaires ever since. As the representative for the British colony who gathered there, Lord Brougham soon made his opinion known and his advice was often sought by the town's administrators, advice which he gave willingly, flattered by the attention paid to him. When the municipality asked him to appeal to the French government over some economic problem, he addressed himself directly to Louis-Philippe calling him 'mon ami', an appeal which brought the desired result. He gave very helpful advice, too, toward making Cannes an important tourist resort. Not that he was always in agreement with the administration. In 1848 the fancy took him to enter the French Assemblé Nationale as deputy for Grasse. The Ministry of Justice had to remind him that he could only do so if he lost his British nationality. He was, in fact, one of that great race not uncommon in the nineteenth century, an amiable eccentric. On his death in 1868 Cannes gave him a funeral worthy of royalty, while in 1886 the centenary of his birth was marked by the unveiling of his statue.

Today Cannes is still one of the most prestigious of holiday resorts, with international regattas, battles of flowers and the fête du mimosa in February. Flower festivals are an important feature of this part of Provence. The most brilliant artistic event of the year, however, is the International Film Festival in May, when the film world and associated celebrities converge on Cannes. Its renowned Boulevard de la Croisette stretches from the old port in a two-mile curve to Palm Beach, haunt of the rich, with its casino and smart restaurants. It is an esplanade along which one can never tire of idling, bordered, on one side by palm trees and beautiful gardens, on the other by long, sandy beaches. Across the Boulevard luxury hotels follow one upon the other, including the majestic Carlton and the Palais des Festivals et des Congrès. At the western end of la Croisette the harbour, both for pleasure yachts and fishing boats, is always animated. It is dominated by the old town which is grouped on the heights of Mont Chevalier — more often known as le Souquet — the heart of which is the Place de la Castre. The ancient castrum de

Canois is known to have been inhabited both by Ligurians and Romans, some vestiges still remain of its fortifications.

The church of Nôtre-Dame de l'Esperance is in Gothic Provençal style. Nearby is a little Roman chapel, the great square seventeenth-century Cour de Souquet, an ancient watch tower, and the Musée de la Castre which houses an important archeological and ethnographical collection. The old town looks across to the Iles de Lérins which can be reached from Cannes; the boat takes fifteen minutes to Ste. Marguerite and thirty minutes to St. Honorat. Both are fascinating and should not be missed if a visit can be fitted in.

Detour

As one approaches the landing stage of Ste. Marguerite, the great fortress rises up, built by Richelieu, enlarged by the Spaniards when they held the island, and reinforced by the great military architect, Vauban. Here the celebrated 'Man in the Iron Mask', made famous by the novel of Alexandre Dumas, was incarcerated. The much discussed question of his identity remains a mystery. We only know that he indeed existed. One enters Fort Royal by a monumental doorway. In the prison a number of Protestant ministers were held after the Edict of Nantes was revoked, but the great curiosity, of course, is the cell where the man in the iron mask was confined, with its thick walls and triple-barred windows. These isles have been known since antiquity and were described by Pliny, Ste. Marguerite was called in the past Lero in memory of a Ligurian hero to which a temple was consecrated. Excavations round the fortress have revealed important vestiges of houses as well as paintings, mosaics and ceramics dating back to around the year 3 B.C. Most of the island is covered by forest where paths lead through alleys of giant eucalyptus, expanses of heather fragrant with thyme and rosemary, and a great diversity of pine trees. It was here that the monks of St. Honorat used to retire to meditate.

The smaller outer isle of St. Honorat owes its name to the saint who crossed from the mainland at the end of the fourth century and founded a monastery here, a refuge from the turbulent strife of the Middle Ages. Numerous were the pilgrims who came to make, bare-footed, a tour of the island and many celebrated Italians as well as French were buried in the monastery. In 660 St. Aygulphe made it a Benedictine order.

The decadence of the monastery began in the eighth century when it suffered frequent raids from Saracen pirates and Genoise corsairs, gradually it developed more as a stronghold than a place of prayer. So little favourable to a monastic life did it become that in 1788 it was closed and sold during the Revolution. Less than a century later, however, it was returned to the Church. Today, therefore, a part of the island belongs to the monastery. The monks, as well as acting as guides to visitors, tend their vineyards and distil their own liqueur — Lérina. In 1073 a fortress was built to shelter the monks from invaders. The past seems very present in a visit to this imposing sanctuary, rising almost sheer from the Mediterranean. By a flight of stone steps one reaches the cloister, surrounding a square courtyard in the centre of which is a rainwater tank of Roman origin. The upper gallery, supported by white marble columns, leads to the chapel known as Le Saint des Saints — the Holy of Holies — on account of the many sacred relics that it shelters. The modern monastery, built in the nineteenth century, is occupied by the monks and not open to visitors.

Detour II

Ten miles north of Cannes lies Grasse, world centre of the perfume industry. There are some thirty factories around Grasse, of which a few can be visited. At the famous Fragonard perfumery one can watch the arrival of the flowers, primarily roses and jasmin, and their distillation. A fête du Jasmin takes place each July.

Juan-les-Pins

Resorts run one into the other all along this coast — Cannes, Golfe Juan, Juan-les-Pins and Antibes. Golfe Juan, apart from its good beaches, is of little interest except that here Napoleon landed on his return from Elba. Just inland lies Vallauris, a pottery centre since before the Romans, but made famous more recently by Picasso, whose workshop was in the Fabrique Madoura.

Juan-les-Pins, however, is an elegant resort with tree-lined avenues, luxury hotels and a popular casino. One can walk from here along the pleasant Route des Sables to Cap d'Antibes which has a good beach known as the Plage du Sallis. From here you can explore the Cap along the sands and climb the light-house and observation platform with a marvellous view over the Baie des Anges.

La Garoupe

Down below the little resort of La Garoupe is very animated, with a delightful boating harbour for children. The Sanctuary de Garoupe is of fine wrought-

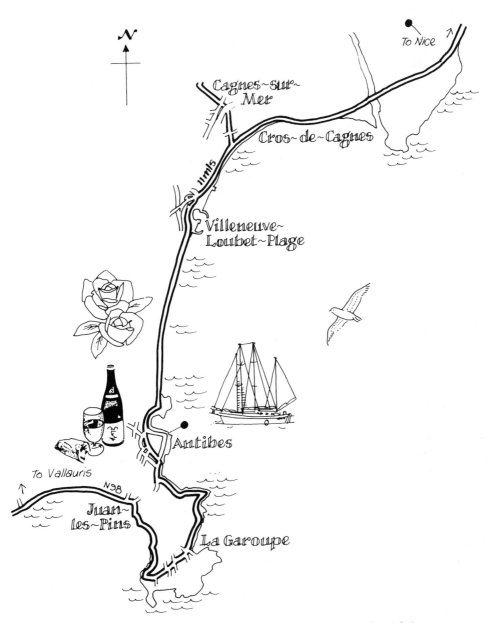

iron, while the interior consists of two parallel chapels each with its own nave. The largest has modern frescoes. The smaller, dating to 1779, has a splendid Russo-Byzantine reredos, thought to be fourteenth century. In the smaller nave is also the gilt statue of Nôtre-Dame de Bon Port, patron saint of sailors for this is above all a sailors' sanctuary. On the first or second Thursday of July the statue of Nôtre-Dame is carried down by fishermen to the cathedral at

Antibes; it is carried back on the following Sunday. The procession attracts large crowds as it is one of the few traditional acts of faith remaining on a coast famous for fashionable beaches and luxury marinas.

Antibes

Smaller than the more fashionable resorts of Cannes and Nice, Antibes has managed to keep much of its individual character, with the narrow streets of its old town and a colourful daily market. Dominating the walled harbour is the imposing Fort Carrée, which is all that remains of the fortifications built by Vauban. The kings of France were well aware of the dangerous position of the town close to the Franco-Savoyard frontier in the fourteenth century. The structure of the twelfth-century castle which Henri IV acquired from the Grimaldis is that of a Roman castrum. Partly reconstructed in the sixteenth century, it is interesting to visit and includes a fine archeological collection, as the beginnings of Antibes, like so much of Provence, go back to antiquity. It was occupied by the Greeks in the fourth century. They called it Antipolis (the town opposite), a reminder of its situation facing across the bay to Nice. Roman occupation followed the Greeks until the barbarian invasions which destroyed the city. Also housed in the Grimaldi castle is a Musée Picasso, which displays marvellous paintings, numerous ceramics and lithographs. Mention should also be made of the church — which was a cathedral in the Middle Ages when its square, twelfth-century tower was used to serve as a watchtower. The interior has a fine sixteenth-century reredos by Louis Bréa and a splendid sculptured sixteenth-century Crucifixion.

The great industry of Antibes is roses, you will see row upon row of greenhouses stretching away into the distance. Here the ever popular Peace was created in 1945 by Francis Meilland. Today one rose in every three is a Meilland. The rosaries of the Domaine de St. André were started by his father, Antoine, who, as a boy, had been more interested in the roses in the neighbouring garden than in the vegetables of his father's market garden. Such was his enthusiasm that the owner of the roses advised his parents to send him to a friend who was a horticulturist, good advice that they followed. The young Antoine spent four years there. In 1939 Francis created a very beautiful yellow rose which he called Antoine Meilland and sent to a fellow rosarist, Robert Pyle, in America. Then war was declared and it was not until five years later that he heard that the precious cuttings that Pyle had planted had all taken and proved an outstanding success.

Lunch at **L'Oursin**, Antibes.

Baie des Anges

Between Antibes and Cagnes-sur-Mer is a four-mile stretch that runs beside a narrow, pebbly beach that is of little interest until one comes to Villeneuve-Loubet-Plage and the great modern complex of Marina Baie des Anges whose construction was as controversial as that of Port Grimaud. Designed by the architect André Minangoy, it is considered one of the most prestigious luxury blocks on the Côte d'Azur, surrounding a swimming pool, a yacht harbour and shopping centre. Others consider this mass of concrete inappropriate in the admirable site of the Baie des Anges.

Cagnes really consists of three towns, the admirable Haut-des-Cagnes, Cagne-ville, which is residential and commercial, and the Cros-de-Cagnes which is a little resort and fishing village. It adjoins St. Laurent-du-Var which, until 1860, used to constitute the frontier until the Comté de Nice was united with France. On the other side of the river is Nice airport which has twice weekly flights to Heathrow.

Nice

I suggest visiting this immense town tomorrow, which enables us to reach Menton by the Upper Corniche, returning tomorrow by the coast road where all the resorts are situated. Between Nice and Menton the mountains come down almost to the sea. Three roads run parallel, the lower, middle and upper corniche. For the Upper Corniche one leaves Nice by the Place Max Baral, but it is well signposted. The road has an excellent surface with spectacular views all the way along the rugged coastline.

Eze

It takes one past the perched village of Eze, one of the most curious of the Côte d'Azur, high up on its lofty pinnacle of rock, an eagle's nest indeed where the Ligurians, the first occupants, made an impregnable refuge from the frequent invasions of pirates. After the Ligurians, it was occupied in turn by Phoenicians, Romans and Saracens. As for its name, tradition holds that it was

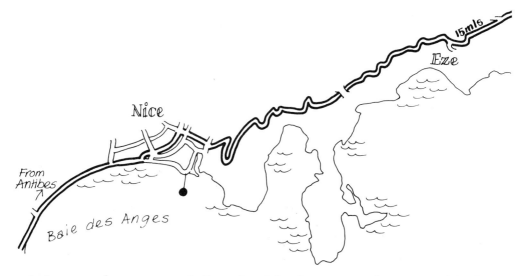

in honour of a sanctuary dedicated to Isis who was greatly venerated in this Graeco-Roman world. The entry to the old village is by a double fortified gate of the fourteenth century. The narrow streets wind up, past shops and artists studios, scattered with flights of steps. Each corner has a special charm, be it a fountain, a crucifixion or a glimpse through an archway to the sea. Nearly at the top is the Chapelle des Penitents Blanc, a simple little fourteenth-century sanctuary.

For the past quarter of a century its overwhelming attraction has been the marvellous exotic gardens, contained within the ramparts of the ruins of the ancient fortress. Following a decision by the municipal council in 1959, the gardens were created by M. Gastan who was responsible for those of Monaco. But the Eze gardens are considered unique in their variety, a riot of every kind of cactus and plants from semi-desert regions, enriched each year by new arrivals, all in a dazzling decor of stones and rocks of every colour.

The little borough suffered numerous vicissitudes down the ages, with invasions by barbaric tribes, uprisings and battles. Yet like a Phoenix re-born from its ashes, its proud emblem of Mariendo Renascor, Eze survived even the summer of 1986 when forest forest fires ravaged the area.

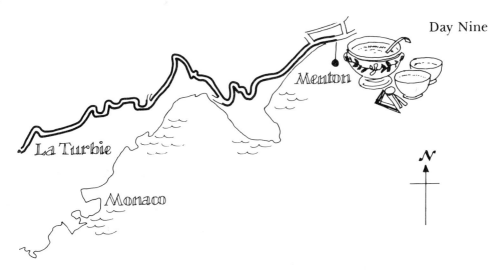

La Turbie

Another two miles brings us to another hilltop village, that of La Turbie, the ancient boundary between Gaul and Italy. In times past turbulent Ligurian tribes constantly menaced communications between Rome and her possessions across the Alps. In order to make his authority respected, Augustus was engaged in numerous campaigns from 25–14 B.C., bringing under his control this region of the Alpes Martimes with, for capital, Cimiez at Nice. To commemorate this achievement the celebrated Trophée des Alpes was erected in the year 6 B.C., a masterpiece of Roman art. It has been submitted to much reconstruction, serving at one time as a Guelph fort and partly blown up on the orders of Louis XIV. However, it is still a tremendously impressive monument commanding an unforgettable view over the principality of Monaco in her bay of Hercules.

Menton

Queen Victoria liked Menton and she probably still would, with its splendid yacht harbour, excellent shops and beautiful gardens in a spectacular backdrop of mountains. Not the least of its claims is that it is the warmest and most sheltered resort on the coast, where oranges and lemons flourish, its *fête des citrons*, during the first week of Lent is one of the most animated events on the Riviera.

The origins of Menton are obscure, although archeologists have found that it was inhabited in the paleolithic age. Her more recent history is the history of

Monaco when, in the thirteenth century, the Grimaldis acquired it together with Roquebrune, thus Menton suffered the many vicissitudes of the Principality including pitched battles between Guelphs and Ghibellines (rival factions), the Grimaldis were partisans of the Guelphs, both were from Genoa. In the French Revolution the Grimaldis lost their sovereignty for twenty-two years, although after the restoration the reigning princes were so utterly tyrannical that in 1848 Menton and Roquebrune rebelled. Both became independent republics until 1840 when they voted for union with France.

The inscription in the Town Hall of Menton — Artium Civitas — shows her ambition to achieve a name in the world of culture. This is shown in a biannual International Art Festival which unites contemporary painting, sculpture, ceramics and tapestry. While for the Festival of Chamber Music, held in August, music lovers from all over the world converge on Menton. It is held on the Parvis of St. Michael, where the coat of arms of Monaco are designed in a mosaic of grey and white pebbles. The whole decor is a delight of Italian charm and fantasy, looking out over the sea.

Of her monuments, the église St. Michael is considered the most beautiful and the most vast baroque church of the region. After admiring its splendid façade, one is seized by the sumptuous baroque decor of the interior, specially remarkable being the beautiful reredos of St. Nicolas in the first of the side chapels and the monumental organ.

Two museums well deserve a visit: the Musée Jean Cocteau, which is housed in a seventeenth-century bastion built by a prince of Monaco, and the Musée du Palais Carnolea housed in the eighteenth-century summer residence of the princes of Monaco. It holds a fine collection of contemporary artists, including Dufy, and numerous modern works gleaned from the exhibits of the International Festival of Art.

It is good, too, to idle in the Rue St. Michel, reserved for pedestrians, as far as the delightful Place aux Herbes, paved with pebbles, shaded by plane trees, in the centre a fountain, just such a square that one has come to recognise as so typical of Provence.

Dinner and overnight at the **Méditerranée**, Menton.

L'Oursin
16 Rue de la République
Antibes
Tel: (93) 34 13 46

This is a particularly good fish restaurant with every variety of fish and seafood.

Closed: August

LA BONNE AUBERGE
Quartier de la Brague
Antibes
Tel: (93) 33 36 65

For a really slap-up meal in a luxurious setting, this celebrated restaurant boasts 2 Michelin stars. It is in Provençal style with a delightful, flower-decked terrace. Specialities include: *Daurade grillé* and *Aile de volaille aux coulis de tomates*. Wine: Côteaux d'Aix.

Closed: 15 November to 15 December

Méditerranée
5 Rue de la République
Menton
Tel: (93) 28 25 25

A large, centrally situated hotel.

Rooms:	90
Facilities:	Restaurant, conference hall, car park
Credit cards:	Diner's Club, Visa
Food:	A large choice of dishes
Wine:	Côtes de Provence
Rating:	★★

PRINCESS ET RICHMOND
617 Promenade de Soleil
Menton
Tel: (93) 35 80 20

A very comfortable hotel, centrally situated but unfortunately without a main restaurant.

Closed:	November 4th to December 20th
Rooms:	44
Facilities:	car park
Credit cards:	American Express, Diner's Club
Food:	Only breakfast is served in the restaurant, but in the evening they are happy to bring a light meal to your room.
Rating:	★★★

Day 10

From Menton to Vence: approx. 35 miles.

Only three miles from Menton is the millionaires' resort of Roquebrune-Cap-Martin, while another three miles on again brings us to Monaco, in a near perfect setting. The Principality has much of interest, including its beautiful palace, prehistoric grottos and the finest oceanic museum in Europe. Monte Carlo, of course, is famed for its casino.

Twelve miles from Monaco brings us to Beaulieu-sur-Mer, appropriately named for it is in a beautiful situation, looking across to the peninsula of St. Jean-Cap-Ferrat.

Like all resorts frequented by the wealthy it has a number of first class restaurants. After Villefranche-sur-Mer, with its picturesque harbour, we dip down into Nice with the most splendid of all splendid views over the Baie des Anges.

Time must dictate what one visits, but at the heart is the Place Massena while, to my mind, nowhere compares with the *vieille ville* as the old quarter is called.

Leaving Nice by the coast road as far as Cagnes-sur-Mer, the D18 should be taken to climb up to Vence.

Breakfast at Menton.

Roquebrune

Only three miles from Menton is Roquebrune-Cap-Martin where luxurious villas look out on thickets of mimosa, giant pines and scattered rocks. For this has always been a millionaires' resort, a favourite in times past with the Empress Eugéné. The village covers all of the peninsula, where only the ruins remain of the Basilica St. Martin, destroyed by pirates in 1400. Roquebrune is one of the most accessible of the perched villages.

Leaving the car in the Parking, a steep flight of steps leads to the medieval village, with its long arched alleys, its numerous staircases and houses hewn out of rock. Continue up to the oldest feudal keep in France, dating from the tenth century. A flight of steps leads up to the first floor, in times past the Salle des Ceremonies. The second floor was the ancient prison, the third the residence of the seigneurs with the dining hall, a primitive kitchen and the sleeping quarters. From the fourth floor, the ancient artillery platform, one looks down over the old brown roofs of the village, Cap-Martin and Monaco. August 5th is the occasion of a traditional procession, representing scenes from the Passion executed in the same way as when it first began in 1467 after a vow made during an epidemic of the plague. Another ceremony takes place on the eve of Good Friday, called the Procession du Christ Mort, instituted by the Pénitents Blancs. A cortège of some sixty people process through the streets, carrying a statue of Christ.

Monte Carlo

To many motoring enthusiasts the name of Monte Carlo is synonymous with

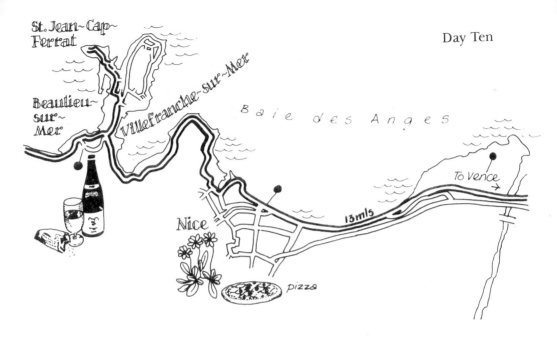

the world famous rally. To the average holidaymaker it means the equally famous casino. Monaco has always been a popular resort, with marvellous beaches, while remaining one of the most pricey. The casino of Monte Carlo is in a near-perfect setting, rising majestically at the end of a beautifully-planned terrace and gardens. Although it was the then reigning Prince Charles III (after whom Monte Carlo is called) who originally authorised the opening of the gaming rooms — in order to augment his revenue — it was Monsieur Blanc, previously director of the casino at Bad Homburg, who really put the casino on its feet. Although it eventually achieved tremendous success, its beginnings were hazardous, so much so that he had even to run a free coach service to attract visitors there from other towns along the coast.

Whilst Monte Carlo owes its reputation to the casino, there is much else besides in the Principality. For music lovers there is a good variety of concerts, ballet and opera, held in the charmingly baroque hall known as the Salle Garnier. It has its full share of night life and restaurants, its cafés as animated as any other resort's on the coast. The national art gallery has a fine collection of French, Flemish and Italian works, including a number of Van Goghs, and a magnificent tenth century Brussels tapestry. The town of Monaco itself, which is the seat of government, has quite another kind of fascination, with quaint old streets and a fine cathedral built in the white stone of La Turbie. The prehistoric grottos have a wealth of stalagmites and stalactites. There are exotic gardens too, with superb view-points and cliffside paths which lead to an oceanographic museum and aquarium which are without equal in Europe. The two towns which comprise the principality, those of Monaco-ville and Monte Carlo are built each on a rocky promontory joined by La Condamine which is the port and commercial district down in the Valley. It is a pity to admire no more than the outside of the Palace where the changing of the guard draws big crowds at midday, for the interior really is worth visiting, dating in some parts back to the thirteenth century, in others to the fifteenth and greatly restored in the nineteenth in the style of the Italian Renaissance. The rose-coloured frescoes that decorate the galleries of the courtyard of honour are of breath-taking beauty.

Although Monaco is known to have been occupied since prehistoric times, later a Phocaean foundation, followed by a Roman port, it was not until the founding of the Grimaldi dynasty in the fourteenth century that she first took her place in history. After the Napeolonic wars its independence was confirmed by the treaty of Vienna, allowing the dynasty to continue thereafter.

Beaulieu

Five miles from Monaco, Beaulieu is one of the most beautiful and much painted places of the Riveira. Surrounded by hills, snug in its bay, a riot of flowers in the gardens of its villas and throughout, the village is a feast of colour. One should visit the Villa Kerylos which is an extremely interesting reproduction of a sumptuous Greek mansion from the time of Pericles, conceived by archeologists. No expense has been spared, with splendid marble and alabaster, exotic wood and frescoes that are reproductions of models taken from antiquity. The wood of the furniture is all inlaid with ivory, bronze and leather, copied from illustrations and mosaics. While from the many windows there are views over the Bay of Fourmis and across to Eze and Cap Ferrat. No imagination has been spared either in the beauty of the gardens which surround the villa.

Lunch at **The Reserve**, Beaulieu.

St. Jean-Cap-Ferrat

After lunching here, we cross to the peninsula of St. Jean-Cap-Ferrat, where, at the extreme tip, is Cap Ferrat which gave its name to the peninsula. On its east, the narrow promontory of St. Hospice takes its name from St. Auspicius who settled here in the sixth century. At its angle with the principle part of the peninsula is the little fishing village of St. Jean, renowned for the colony of writers who have for long made it their home. Baroness Rothschild founded the Fondation Ephrussi de Rothschild, a beautiful villa in an incomparable setting in the narrowest part of the peninsula. It houses the Musée Ile de France which has a magnificent collection of art including works of Monet, Renoir and Sisley, sixteenth- and seventeenth-century Flemish tapestries and splendid porcelain.

Villefranche-sur-Mer

On the other side of the peninsula from Beaulieu, Villefranche-sur-Mer has a very different charm. But charm it has of the very first order, a marvellous little fishing port flanked by the brown-roofed village, whose narrow alleys have preserved all their medieval character. The little baroque church of St. Michel has a curious multi-coloured statue of St. Roch and his dog and a fine eighteenth-century organ. While the Chapelle St. Pierre is of particular interest since in 1957 it was entirely redecorated by Jean Cocteau.

It strikes me as being one of the rare places on this coast that has conceded little to commercialism, for since Roman days Villefranche was always a naval harbour. In the eighteenth century the Piedmontese held a fleet here to keep down the Barbarians and other Corsairs.

Nice

Soon after leaving Villefranche one rounds the Mont Boron to dip down into Nice, with a tremendous view over the Baie des Anges. Whether you find Nice too large, too noisy or too popular, it cannot be ignored. The perfect way of seeing it is after dark — to see the lights glittering all the way across the Baie des Anges is fabulous.

Its name comes from the Greek Nikaia, meaning 'victory', a significant attribute for its situation, since the dawn of history, has always been greatly coveted. At a much earlier date the hill of Cimiez was a citadel, occupied by Ligurian tribes. Then came the Etruscans over whom the Phocaeans were victorious. After the Greeks came the Romans until the sixth century when their settlement was destroyed by Barbarian invasions. From the tenth century she flourished anew with the domination of the Counts of Provence. In the fourteenth century, however, came more trouble when Louis d'Anjou and the Prince of Naples made rival claims, whereupon the Count of Savoy took the opportunity to step in, having first assured the complicity of the town's governor. According to all accounts he brought prosperity and with only the occasional incident, common to all frontier towns, Nice lived peacefully under the rule of Savoy until being united with France in 1860. With so many diverse races battling for domination it is no wonder that her population adopted the light-hearted temperament that is evident in her throbbing vitality.

In the past, as in Cannes, it was the winter months that the wealthy spent at Nice, their visit often culminating with the festivities of the Carnival. Although February is no longer a holiday month and the seasons have changed, the tradition nonetheless remains. For the fortnight before Shrove Tuesday holidaymakers converge on Nice to watch or partake in the frolic: processions, with superlatively decorated *chars*, bands beating, and great giants, enormous masked figures that are one of the chief features. There are balls too, firework displays, horse races and battles of flowers.

Like all big cities there is, of course, more than one Nice.

The magnificent Promenade des Anglais, the most celebrated esplanade in the world, stretches the whole way along the sea front and it has its full quota of the elderly who retire here to warm their rheumatic bones in the sun. Across the road, with an avenue of palms and oleander down the centre, are the palace-type hotels still striving to guard something of their past splendour, like the massive Negresco, baroque of the Belle Epoch. The glamour of Nice is wearing thinner today, but its popularity had a long innings. Since holidays with pay were introduced in 1935 Nice was the tradition. The Côte d'Azur meant Nice. The name of the avenue was no chance choice. Until 1820 this part of the coast was difficult to reach and it was the large English colony here who undertook the expense of the construction of a road alongside the sea. Almost at the end of this Promenade des Anglais is the delightful Jardin Albert, pleasant gardens with a fountain and plenty of shade. Behind is the Place Massena, with its pink stucco houses and arcades, which might be called the centre of modern Nice. The immense coach station is not far distant. The name of the square commemorates one of her two great sons, Massena, who was born in 1758 of Jewish parents and was one of the most distinguished

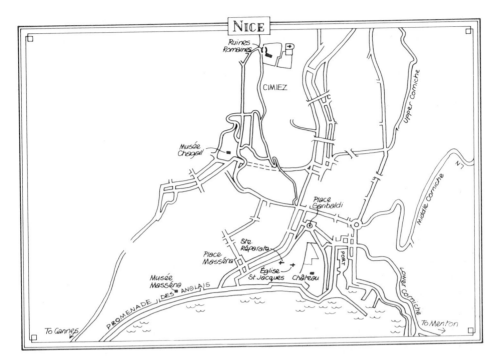

leaders of the Napoleonic wars, created Maréchal de France by the Emperor. Her other great son was Garibaldi, born here in 1807, an ardent patriot and revolutionary who did much to bring about a united Italy.

The Promenade des Anglais continues into the Quai des Etats Unis, round the corner of which is the port, a long rectangular harbour where fishing smacks and leisure boats bob side by side, bordered by streets on three sides with their quota of small restaurants. It is dominated by the château, now a pleasant almost circular garden set on the hill top, on the site of the château fortress which was destroyed at the beginning of the eighteenth century. A few ruins remain of the ancient cathedral which also stood here.

Until relatively recently the flower and vegetable market were together in the old quarter. Now, however, the flower market is separate, held in the Rue St. François-de-Paule and open all day, whereas the vegetable market, which is quite fascinating, is only open in the mornings.

To my mind nowhere in Nice compares with the *vieille ville* which one reaches by the delightful Place Garibaldi lined with eighteenth-century houses in ochre stone. There one engages in a labyrinth of colourful alleys with high houses across which washing flaps in the breeze. There are ill-paved steps down and steep streets up, an occasional archway and shops selling wares of every kind. Restaurants to suit every purse spill on to the narrow pavements. You can take your choice between steaming fish soup or a *salade Niçoise* or settle yourself in a Pizzeria and watch the pizzas being made in front of you, remembering that here the population is as much Italian as French.

Of the numerous museums and churches, there is the cathedral, dedicated to St. Reparate, the patron saint of the city, which stands out from afar with her magnificent tiled dome. The interior is baroque in style, highly ornamental, with a fine frieze and beautiful seventeenth-century woodwork. Nearby is the seventeenth-century Palais Lascaria which has an interesting reconstruction of an eighteenth-century pharmacy with a fine collection of recipients. A monumental staircase leads up to the reception rooms. The church of St. Jacques is of slightly earlier date than the cathedral, built on the site of an ancient chapel. The interior is majestic, the side chapels having loggias which used to be reserved for the nobility. The sacristy, or vestry, should not be missed for the massive walnut cupboards are admirable, one of them contains the church's treasure. The Chapel de la Misericorde, not always open, has a masterpiece of fifteenth-century Niçois art in the beautiful reredos. The Church of St. Martin St. Augustin is the ancient parish church of Nice, where Garibaldi was baptised and Martin Luther celebrated Mass in 1510. The Eglise Nôtre-Dame de l'Assomption is also ancient, built in the fifteenth century. It holds a very beautiful Pieta, an early work of Louis Bréa and his arresting Crucifixion.

Of the museums, the Musée Massena is so called because it is housed in the mansion built in the nineteenth century by the Maréchal's great-grandson. It has a wide variety of exhibits including furniture and Niçois naifs, beautiful Renaissance silver and much of the town's folklore and history. The Musée des Beaux-Arts has a very rich art collection, some of which is consecrated to the extreme orient as well as a marvellous number of Impressionists and earlier work. There is even a collection of Picasso's ceramics. For contemporary artists there is the Musée Marc Chagall, holding the most important permanent collection of his work in the world.

There are other museums and churches too, but above all one should go up to the archeological site of Cimiez, the ancient Roman capital where excavations have revealed an immense number of early sites, including a thermal establishment, a residential district with paved alleys, a baptistry, a fifth-century Christian basilica and a first-century amphitheatre.

Most of the excavations are housed in a beautiful seventeenth-century Italian building close to the town's ancient rival, the Roman Cemenelum, with a fine collection of objects that were in daily use: ceramics and glasses, jewellery and tools, documents and statues. There are also Etruscan, Greek and Italian exhibits and a pleasant garden, shaded and gay with hollyhocks.

Vence

Leaving Nice on the coast road as far as Cagnes-sur-Mer, the D36 should be taken to Vence. You could stop off at St. Paul de Vence, ever-popular with artists, perched like an eagle's nest looking across to sea and mountains. The ramparts, built in the sixteenth century are almost intact. Stop to admire a coat-of-arms or bronze knocker on the ancient cobbled streets or visit the remarkable Maeght Foundation's contemporary exhibits.

Dinner and overnight at **Hotel Florida**, Vence.

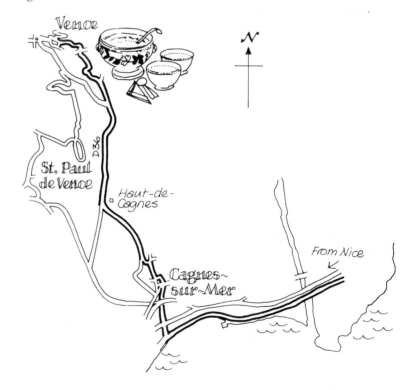

La Réserve
Boulevard Mar.-Leclerc
Beaulieu-sur-Mer
Tel: (93) 01 00 01

This luxurious restaurant, with a Michelin star, has a delightful terrace overlooking the sea. Its specialities include *Feuilletede de homard aux blettes* and marvellous *Beignets de fraise au coulis de framboise*. Its recommended wines are Bandol and Gassin.

Hotel Florida
438 Boulverad Emm. Maurel
Vence

This pleasant hotel provides you with a very friendly reception. The restaurant provides well-varied menus.

CHATEAU DU DOMAINE ST.-MARTIN
Route de Coursegoules
Vence
Tel: (93) 58 02 02

This top luxury hotel is set in a delightful park.

Closed:	20th November until beginning March
Rooms:	14, and 10 villas
Facilities:	Swimming pool, tennis courts, parking, restaurant
Food:	With a Michelin star, its specialities include a *Ragout de pâtés aux truffes fraîches* and *Filets de rougets verdurette*
Wines:	Bellet, Cassis
Credit cards:	American Express, Diner's Club, Eurocard, Visa
Rating:	★★★★★

NICE: USEFUL INFORMATION

Tourist Office:	Avenue Thiers
	Tel: (93) 87 07 07
Population:	338486
Facilities:	Airport, rail and coach stations, golf course, water sports

VENCE: USEFUL INFORMATION

Tourist Office:	Place Gd-Jardin
	Tel: (93) 58 06 38
Population:	13428
Facilities:	Hotels, camp site

Day 11

Vence to Levens: approx. 150 miles.

The ancient city of Vence, sheltered by the impressive range of the Baous repays exploration before setting off northwards. After crossing the Col de Vence, a slight detour can be made to Barnabé, otherwise we will continue on to Gréolières-les-Neiges, a popular winter sports resort, and the once important village of Roquestéron then down to Le Broc and Gattières.

After lunch, we discover the beautiful valley of the Vésubie and the national park of the Mercantour, then down to Levens.

Vence — Rue du Marché

Breakfast at Vence.

Entering the *vieille ville* from the Grand Jardin one is at once in its very heart, the Place du Peyra with its much painted fountain in the form of an urn, fed by the source of the Foux. In fact, in times past this square was a Roman forum and the old city has preserved all its medieval atmosphere. From here a long, narrow alley, lined with stalls of colourful fruit and vegetables, leads to the Place Clemenceau and the cathedral. Built between the eleventh and thirteenth centuries, the chief interest of this massive monument are the beautiful fifteenth-century choir stalls. Nearby is the Place Godeau, named after her most celebrated bishop who, in the seventeenth century, not only restored the cathedral, then in a piteous condition, but made the town prosperous by introducing a number of handicrafts, including leatherwork, perfumery and pottery.

If this is a Spring visit, you will discover one of the wonders of Provence: that while in Vence and Tourrettes, nevertheless 1000m. up, the air is already warm and the flowerbeds gay with cyclamen and primulas. However, leaving Vence to the north on the D2, once over the Col de Vence snow will still be thick upon the ground.

A slight detour should be made to the delightful little village of St. Barnabé after which we pass close to Courségoules, with its high brown houses striding up the white hillside.

144

Gréolières

Gréolières, a perched village, is worth visiting for the beautiful thirteenth-century reredos in its church and a twelfth-century sculptured Virgin. This brings us to Gréolières-les-Neiges, a popular winter sports centre fourteen miles from Vence and, at 1,600m. the most southerly ski station of the Alps. For country lovers it is also a marvellous region, with splendid walks and a multitude of alpine flowers. From the summit of the Cheiron, reached by teleski, one has a superb panorama across the Alps and to Italy.

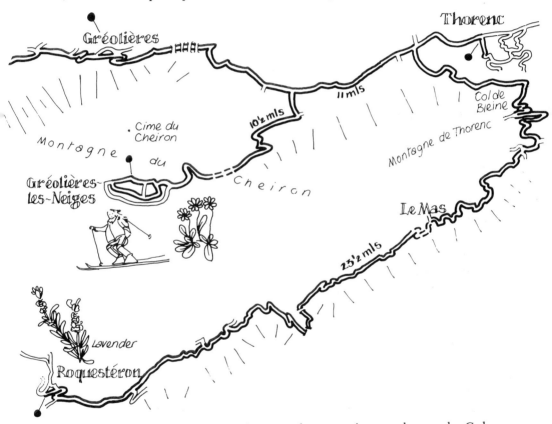

From Gréolières we continue on to Thorenc, there turning north over the Col de Bleine, through le Mas to Roquestéron where half of the village used to belong to the king of Piedmont, the other to the king of France. Follow the D1 through to Le Broc, yet another perched village with a delightful little square, a fountain and medieval church. A *broc* means a large jug, and the village's coat of arms bears the insignia of a large red jug with the inscription *Qu a begu beura*.

145

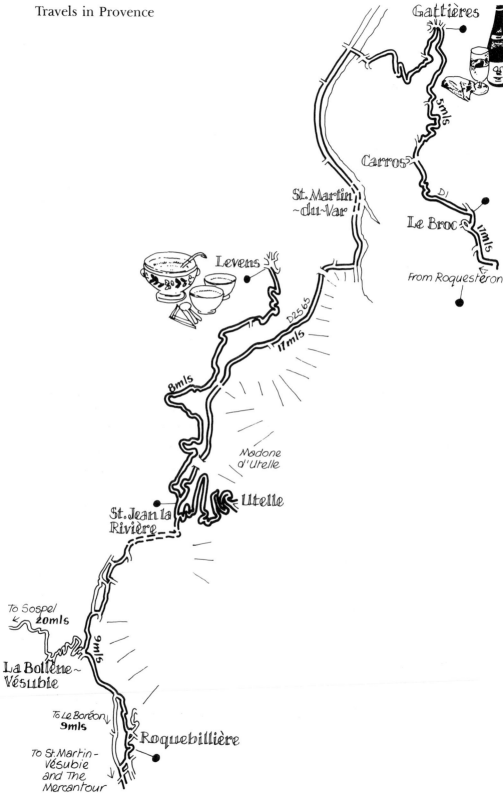

Travels in Provence

Gattières

5mls

Carros

D1

St. Martin
~du~Var

Le Broc

17mls

From Roquestéron

Levens

D2565

17mls

8mls

Madone
d'Utelle

Utelle

St. Jean la
Rivière

To Sospel
20mls

9mls

La Bollène~
Vésubie

To Le Boréon
9mls

Roquebillière

To St.Martin~
Vésubie
and The
Mercantour

Little by little these humble villages have become the haunt of artists, the bistros transformed into restaurants. Yet if, in the process, they lose some of their original simplicity, at least they have escaped the neglect that is so often the fate of those in less favoured regions.

The road on to Gattières is panoramic, a much used description but really no other term applies. The road passes close to the feudal fortress of Carros. Gattières today shows little sign of its historic past when the Dukes of Savoy held it as an important outpost. Like other such villages it has its narrow streets of high houses and a little Roman Gothic church with a remarkable multicoloured sculpture of St. Nicolas.

Lunch at **Hostellerie des Gattières**, Gattières.

From Gattières, we join the N202 for a brief spell, to turn off soon after St. Martin-du-Var on to the D2565 for the beautiful valley of the Vésubie.

Detour

Then, at St. Jean la Rivière, a detour of only a few miles is well worth making to Utelle, reached by what seems an unending series of twists and turns. At 800m. it is a veritable balcony over the valley of the Vésubie and the Alps Maritimes.
In the past its situation made it one of the most important strongholds of the region of which its fortifications bear witness. Ancient houses surround the village square with a delightful fountain and the medieval church of St. Veran whose interior is richly decorated, including a finely carved reredos.
Further on the Madone d'Utelle, founded in the nineteenth century, is the scene of pilgrimages on August 15th and September 8th.

From St. Jean la Rivière the road continues on to Lantosque flanked by snow capped mountains and pervaded by the acrid scent of wood ash, so often prevalent in these mountain villages. Its remoteness is one denied to the better known hillside villages further south.

St.-Martin Vésubie

At the head of the valley St.-Martin Vésubie is an attractive little mountain town with a narrow canal of water running through its main street, so narrow that only pedestrians can penetrate. Rather surprisingly it boasts the record of having been the second town in France to get electric power.

After St.-Martin the road opens out into the wide, alpine scenery of meadows dotted with chalets and, even in Spring, snow piled high at the roadsides, to Le Boréon, a popular winter sports centre.

Mercantour

With Le Boréon we are in the great national park of the Mercantour, one of the most remote and unspoilt parts of Provence, perhaps of the whole of France. Only a century ago all this region was completely isolated, mule tracks that straggled through the mountains were the sole means of communication. The improvement began when Nice was united to France and progressively the network of tracks became roads and opened up the region. The summits of the majestic chain of the Mercantour vary between 2,500 and 3,000m. Yet that of the Grand Capelet, at 2,935m., is less than twenty miles from the sea. Numerous streams and rivers have their source here, the Roya and the Vésubie, the Tinée and the Var. While over two hundred lakes are dotted among the hills, icebound from October until June.

The Mercantour used to be the hunting ground of the kings of Italy and consequently protected. When the Compté of Nice was united with France the Italian minister, Cavour, managed to obtain permission to keep the Mercantour, and consequently the Roya valley which bordered Italy. It was not until a treaty was signed in 1947 that this anomaly was brought to an end by establishing it as a French zone. By 1946, however, the fauna had been virtually annihilated, with only thirty-five mountain goat left and six ibex. Today, happily, it has become a reserve so that the numbers are up to 1,700 wild goats and 1,500 ibex as well as many other species.

Well-traced paths have been made, redolent with the perfume of pine and birch and a paradise of wild flowers. For of the 4,500 species in France, 2,400 are to be found in the Alpes Maritimes.

The reason for this fantastic vegetation is due to the fact that much of the Mercantour, being the most southerly of the important ranges, escaped almost entirely the worst of the great Ice Ages that destroyed the vegetation in other parts of the Alps.

Detour

Returning back down the valley, three miles after Roquebillière one could turn east, through La Bollène-Vésubie, up over the Col de Turini and down to Sospel. An overnight stay at Sospel would allow you to set off early the next morning north to St. Dalmas-de-Tende. There a guide (essential) and jeep can be hired to take you to the Valley of Marvels. Although beyond the scope of this 12-day trip, a day spent in the Valley of Marvels is a fabulous experience, the entry into the most ancient natural history museum in the world. For in this prehistoric sanctuary are the engravings made by primitive man in the age of Bronze, buried by snow between the beginning of October and June. One should be suitably clad, an anorak and strong boots.

The valley has the greatest conglomeration of some hundred thousand engravures, the majority dating back to the age of Bronze, some to the Stone Age. The first inhabitants are thought to have been Ligurian tribes who founded communities five thousand years ago, living by agriculture and cattle-raising. They learned the simple uses of flint and metal so that we see their first tools engraved beside domestic animals. It is thought that these early art forms were primitive man's way of escaping from the terrors of the unknown, symbolic sacrifices to Mont Bego. The traces of a dwelling could have been their way of asking for benediction on their homes. Archeologists conjecture that it may have been a place of pilgrimage, a pagan cult to the glory of Mont Bego. In the Middle Ages this region was greatly feared by shepherds who refused to go there for their summer pasturage. In 1975 an International Congress for the Study of Prehistoric Science voted to protect the site as 'of inestimable value for the study of humanity'.

Levens

Return back down the Vésubie valley and take the D19 to Levens. Levens is a favourite centre for excursions in all directions, with a marvellous view over the Var and the Vésubie. She has even — unusual and paradoxical for so Provençal a village — an Olympic-sized swimming pool. Amongst its ancient houses in the Rue Massena is the Maréchal's family home, dated 1722. Beside the pleasantly shaded gardens is the baroque chapel of the Pénitents Blancs, September 4th is the fête de St. Antonin, with its *saut de boutin*, dancing and *farandoles*.

Dinner and overnight at **La Vignerie**, Levens.

Hostellerie des Gattières
Gattières

Although the *Auberge du Gattières* has for long been reputed, the Hostellerie, just opposite, is less hard on the budget, yet with an excellent menu. Lunch always starts off with a *Cascade d'hors d'oeuvre* and this really does describe the numerous starters, including delicious *Jambon du pays* or smoked mountain ham. A *Côte de Provence* makes a good accompaniment.

La Vigneraie
Levens
Tel: (93) 79 70 46

This is a quiet and comfortable hotel with a shady terrace.

Closed:	1st October to 12th January
Rooms:	18
Facilities:	Restaurant, car park
Credit cards:	Eurocard
Food:	Very good menu at extremely reasonable prices.
Rating:	★★

MALAUSSÉNA
Levens
Tel: (93) 79 70 06

This is a small, comfortable hotel, centrally situated.

Closed:	1st November to 10th December
Rooms:	12
Facilities:	Restaurant
Credit cards:	Eurocard
Rating:	★★

LEVENS: USEFUL INFORMATION

Tourist Office:	Hôtel de Ville
	Tel: (93) 79 70 22
Population:	1800
Altitude:	570 metres

Day 12

Levens to Sisteron: approx. 185 miles.

Levens is a good point from which to set off on this last day since it is only four miles from the N202 in the direction of Castellane and the Route Napoleon via Puget-Théniers and Entrevaux. From Castellane we visit one of the great natural curiosities of France: the Verdon gorges, and the delightful old town of Moustiers-Ste.-Marie.

From here a detour can be made as far as Riez, with its marvellous baptistry. Otherwise we return to Castellane along the north bank of the Verdon. Here we continue north up the Route Napoleon to the ancient city of Digne, today a popular thermal spa in a wonderful mountain setting. You may choose to stop here for the night or continue north to the alpine resort of Château-Arnoux, after which we reach Sisteron on the limit of Provence.

Moustiers-Ste.-Marie

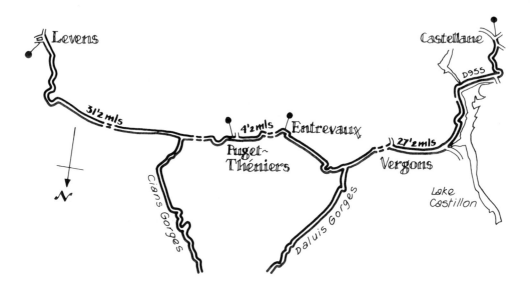

Breakfast at Levens

Follow the N202 north and west to Puget-Théniers.

Detour

One could turn off the N202 up the spectacular Cians Gorges, if you have time. The Cians is a tributary of the Var which it joins after a journey of only fifteen miles from its source, 1,600m. up, which have resulted in these tremendously deeply-cleft gorges, considered among the most impressive in the Alps.

Puget-Théniers

This ancient borough on the banks of the Var was once the capital of the district. It is worth a visit for the site alone, although its church of Nôtre-Dame has some very fine sculpture and a handsome reredos.

Entrevaux

Three miles further on we come to Entrevaux, for long one of the great citadels protecting the Var valley. Only the ruins remain of the château of the Grimaldis, but it strikes one at once as a great military fortress which was later fortified by Vauban. The village, beside the river and at the foot of the great rocky ridge, is situated with an eye to defence like many other villages of this

Var valley. Her seventeenth-century cathedral is in keeping with the general aspect of a stronghold, built into the ramparts and with a crenellated spire. The impressive entrance leads into an interior that astonishes by its richness in so seemingly isolated and unlikely a place.

Nearby are the magnificent Daluis gorges, wildly grandiose, but which time may not permit to see more than a mile or so.

Continuing along the N202 takes us over the Col de Toutes Aures. Then, shortly after Vergons, we turn left on the D955, passing alongside the lake of Castillon, with its spectacular dam, to Castellane, a distance of sixty miles from Levens.

Castellane

Castellane, in the past, was a stronghold of considerable importance, three times besieged and each time unsuccessfully. The old town is typically Provençal, nestling at the foot of 'le Roc' as the great cliff above is called. The Place Marcel Sauvaire is the heart of the town, with cafés and a fountain. It leads into the Rue Nationale where, in the ancient sous-préfecture, it is recorded that Napoleon lunched on March 3rd, 1815. Behind it are medieval streets, with another delightful fountain, known as *La Fontaine aux Lions*, the Tour de l'Horloge and a gateway in the ancient fortifications. Behind the little Roman church of St. Victor, build in the twelfth century, a path leads up to the Chapelle Nôtre-Dame du Roc, built in the seventeenth century. From there we have a very fine view across to the Tour Pentagonale opposite and over Castellane and the entrance to the Verdon Gorges.

For it is from Castellane that we are going to visit one of the great natural curiosities of France.

Grand Canyon du Verdon

Covering a distance of ninety-four miles by road, pages would be needed adequately to describe these grandiose and extraordinary gorges that touch, in places, depths of 3,300 ft. They reproduce on a small scale the Grand Canyon of Colorado, the river flowing through rocks and chasms.

The gorges were first explored by an eminent pot-holer in 1905, when he

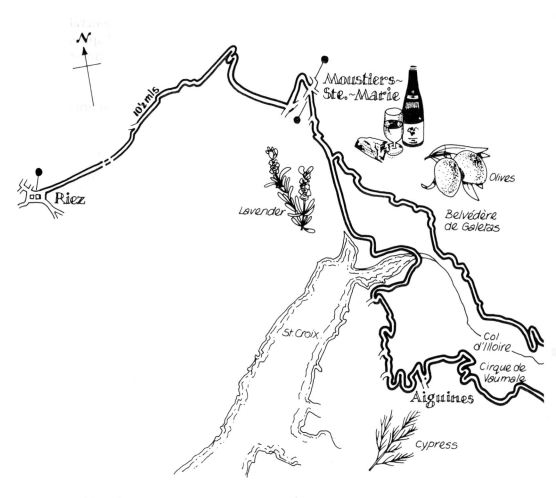

trekked for fourteen miles at great personal risk. In 1928 the Touring Club of France undertook to lay out paths enabling the gorges to be visited on foot without risk. It was not, however, until 1947 that the road along the southern bank of the Verdon was hewn out of the rock and in 1973 the *Route des Crêtes* gave motorists the opportunity to make this round trip.

Leaving Castellane on the D952 the road follows the right bank of the Verdon, a road along which the great cliffs and boulders are imposing from the beginning. A narrow pass hewn out of the rock is called the Porte de St. Jean.

A little further on, at the Pont de Soleils, the road divides, the north bank

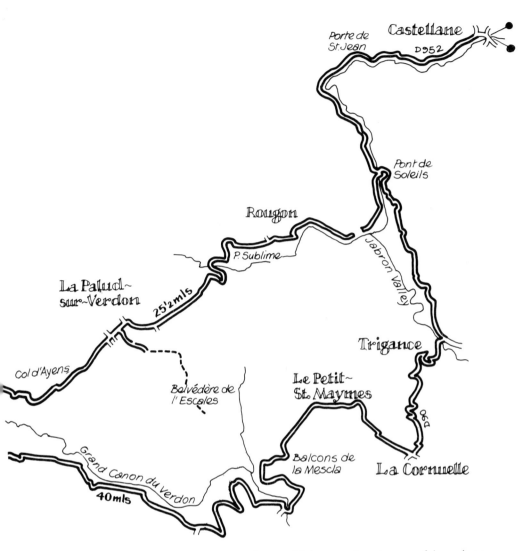

being taken on the return journey. The D955 leaves the river at this point to follow the green valley of the Jabron for four miles, when one turns off on to the D90 for a mile to the perched village of Trigance, with its vast feudal château flanked by four towers. A delightful hotel-restaurant is now housed in the château and there could certainly be few more romantic places to spend a night.

Joining the D71 the road continues on to La Cornuelle from where we look across to the perched village of Comps-sur-Artuby, dominated by its little Gothic chapel of St. André. The road climbs up to Le Petit-St. Maymes, to redescend and climb again to the Balcons de la Mescla. This point is indeed a natural balcony from which we look down, about 250m. into the Mescla, the word 'mescla' meaning *mélange* (or mixing) for here the waters of the Artuby converge with those of the Verdon. It is indeed one of the most impressive sites of the south bank. It is here, too, that the Verdon changes its direction, having hitherto flowed south, it now turns north-west. It is also the beginning of the stretch of road known as the Corniche Sublime.

We cross the Pont de l'Artuby, over a bridge which is a true feat of engineering, built right over the canyon which is sunk, here, between vertical cliffs. The road climbs up again, round the Pilon de Fayet, at a height of 935m., before passing through the two tunnels de Fayet. Between them there is a stopping place from where one has a fabulous view down over the great loop that the Verdon makes at a point called the Etroit des Cavaliers.

We leave the river for three miles before reaching the Falaise (cliff) des Cavaliers which is at the beginning of the Grand Canyon along a length of fifteen miles. One can only describe this road in superlatives, the next two miles, built in 1947, allow one to follow the precipice with gorges between 200-400m. below. From the Pas de l'Imbut the river disappears beneath the great rocks and boulders broken off from the cliffs above. But we leave the gorges again to describe a semi-circle round the wooded Cirque de Vaumale, then up to the culminating point at a height of 1,204m. the Col d'Illoire — where we have a last view, for the present, of the Grand Canyon.

The village of Aiguines, dotted with cypresses, has a fairy-tale castle roofed with glazed tiles and four pepperpot towers. After the village we descend in zig-zags again, looking down on the beautiful lake of Ste. Croix, which the road follows for a short way, through the valley of the Maire, surrounded by fields of lavender, to climb again to Moustiers-Ste.-Marie.

Moustiers-Ste.-Marie

Moustiers, which owes its name to a monastery founded here in the fifth century, has one of the most remarkable situations of Upper Provence, in a breach between two great cliffs which dominate the town. The cliff heads are linked by a wrought-iron chain in the middle of which is a gilt cross. The chain was fastened to the cliffs by the wish of a cavalier returned from the crusades after a long imprisonment. The whole is a delightful labyrinth of narrow streets and tiny squares, arcades and arches, with its Romanesque church, shaded by cypresses, possessing a splendid steeple.

It is well worth taking the nearby pathway, with magnificent views over the village all the way, to the chapel of Nôtre-Dame de Beauvoir. The original chapel was founded in the fifth century, the bishop of Clermont was said to have made a pilgrimage here in the year 470. It was reconstructed in the twelfth century and pilgrimages have continued ever since.

In the seventeenth and eighteenth centuries Moustiers was famed for its glazed earthenware, highly prized by collectors. According to tradition, it was introduced here by a monk from Florence who brought with him the secret of this particularly beautiful workmanship. The earliest ware was decorated in pale blue and, as in Italy, represented scenery where figures were included, often hunting scenes. Sometimes the subjects were mythological with geometrical arabesques. In the eighteenth century Joseph Olerys introduced the Spanish method of multicolour and applied it to small objects of everyday life, birds, flowers and sometimes people in caricature which were very popular.

Every year a long caravan of mules, loaded with their produce, would set off for the celebrated fair at Beaucaire. By the end of the twelfth century, Moustiers had twelve workshops in being, and then the decline set in until, by 1874, no earthenware at all was being made. In 1925, however, one Marcel Provence undertook to get the production going again with the introduction of modern techniques and new designs of Provençal inspiration as well as the traditional patterns. Today the earthenware of Moustiers is proving once again successful. The *Musée de la Faience* is housed in a vast crypt beneath the church, built in the Middle Ages by the monks of Lérins. Each window is consecrated to one of the great craftsmen who was responsible for the glory of Moustiers earthenware during the seventeenth and eighteenth centuries.

Detour

It is well worth travelling another eight miles to Riez, if only for the marvellous fifth-century baptistry which is one of the rare Merovingian monuments still existing in France, comparable to that of Fréjus. Its exterior is square, the interior octagonal. The dome which covers it was restored in the twelfth century. The baptistry now houses a lapidary museum.

Across the road stand four beautiful granite columns, crowned with capitals in white marble, which are all that remain of an ancient Roman temple, dedicated to Apollo, erected in the first century of our era. For Riez possessed a Roman settlement before becoming a bishopric, for centuries it was one of the most important cities of the region.

The old town remains typically Provençal, with its fountain, its square shaded by plane trees and fine seventeenth-century mansions which once belonged to the nobility of the city, including the beautiful Renaissance Hotel de Mazan. It has also two fortified gateways, the Tour de l'Horloge and ruins of its ramparts. The town is dominated by Mont St. Maxime whose part-Roman chapel, once a refuge for pilgrims, has six beautiful Corinthian columns and a splendid panorama over the Alps of Provence. The fifteenth-century Hôtel de Ville, once the episcopal palace, houses the museum 'Nature en Provence' of unusual interest, exhibiting, as it does, everything concerning the nature of the region: fossils and minerals, plants and insects from the prehistoric era up to the present day.

Lunch at **Les Santons**, Moustiers-Ste.-Marie

On leaving Moustiers the scenery is again typical of Provence with olive groves and fields of lavender.

Verdon (north bank)

At the belvedere of Galetas we see the breach where the Verdon emerges from the Grand Canyon. Then, at the belvedere of Mayreste one receives the first overall impression of the gorges seen from this north side.

After the Col d'Ayens, already at a height of 1032m., one follows the deep ravine made by a small tributary of the Verdon, to La Palud-sur-Verdon, a delightful village that is a popular tourist centre. Its little church has, like Moustiers, a handsome twelfth-century Romanesque steeple. It also possesses two pleasant hotel-restaurants.

Two miles after La Palud we reach the gorges again where belvederes follow one after the other, at each, space has been made for motorists to stop to admire the spectacular view — across the gorges and torrents, the Mescla and the ochre cliffs. At the belvedere de l'Escalès, we look down on a path beneath the cliffs which descends vertically. It takes twenty minutes to walk to the Pointe Sublime and back. The car, however, must follow the road which makes a great loop back before winding round to a point where it can be left in the car park of the auberge. From here, it is only a ten minute walk to the Pointe Sublime from where one looks down on the confluence of the Verdon and the Baou and a splendid view across to the beginning of the Grand Canyon. High above the car park is the perched village of Rougon.

Route Napoleon

The road continues to wind and climb back to Castellane where we rejoin the Route Napoleon.

When Napoleon landed at Golfe Juan on March 1st, 1815, the Emperor, with his little group of followers, spent their first night at Cannes. There they learned that he was likely to meet hostility in the Rhône valley, so he decided to take, instead, the road to Grasse in order to reach the valley of the Durance across the Alps. When he took it, the route between Grasse and Castellane was little better than a mule track.

The road was entirely resurfaced and opened in 1932. On the monuments and tablets commemorating this journey, there always figures an eagle with spread wings, Napoleon's symbol inspired by his declaration that 'the eagle will fly from steeple to steeple until he reaches the towers of Nôtre-Dame'. We leave Castellane on the N85 up over the Col de Leque which, at an altitude of 1146m., looks back across Castellane and the lake of Castillon.

Senez

The road drops down through a bleak, arid region, scattered with rocks and boulders and across the river Asse to Senez, dreaming of its past glory. For although, today, it is a little village of less than two hundred inhabitants, as the Gallo-Roman city of Sanitium it was the seat of one of the oldest bishoprics of France, dating back to the fourth century. This explains what appears to be the unusually large proportions of its church for so small a community. The former cathedral, built in the twelfth century, is a beautiful monument, Romano-Provençal in style, with splendid carved choir stalls and reredos and a handsome seventeenth-century lectern. A few miles brings us to Barrême, another small village whose sole claim to fame is an inscription on one of its houses that it was here that Napoleon slept on March 3rd, 1815.

Travels in Provence

Digne

A few miles further on we begin to climb up to the prealps of Digne which, with their bare, rugged summits, is one of the least populated regions of the Alps, where the occasional stream, a small wood or cultivated patch stand out in surprising contrast. The ancient city of Digne is today a popular spa in a wonderful mountain setting, surrounded by fields of lavender. The modern town centres round the wide, plane-lined Boulevard Gassendi, at one end of which is the curious Grande Fontaine, and the Place Charles de Gaulle, where curists and holiday-makers gather on the terraces of its cafés. For Digne is also a good centre for mountaineering.

Restaurants and hotels are numerous, and, after such a lot of driving, you may prefer to stop at Digne for the night (see p. 163) then leave Provence via Sisteron on the following day.

The basilica of Nôtre-Dame du Bourg is one of the most majestic Romanesque churches in Provence. Built between the thirteenth and fourteenth centuries, the elegant entrance is guarded by crouched lions and crowned with an outsize rose. The vast interior is vaulted. The choir, with a much lower ceiling, has fourteenth-century frescoes, in not very good condition, and fragments of mural paintings. In an alcove there is a small altar of the Merovingian epoch. The old city constitutes the *ville haute*, where winding streets with numerous flights of steps lead up to the former cathedral of St. Jerome, built at the end of the fifteenth century, with a belfry added a century later. The municipal museum has much of interest, the ground floor being devoted to archeology and prehistory; the first floor has a fine collection of paintings of the French, Dutch, Flemish and Italian schools. The second floor consists of landscapes of Digne and Provence.

Commercially, it is an important centre of fruit production and also claims to be the capital of the *Alpes de la lavande*. On the first Saturday and Sunday of August there is a *corso fleuri*, a procession of every kind of vehicle decorated with flowers. While in September the lavender market shows the importance of this industry. For although one associates Grasse in particular with its cultivation, lavender is, of course, characteristic all over Provence. In the nineteenth century it used to be gathered where it grew wild, in bare places where little else flourished. At the beginning of the present century the first fields of cultivated lavender appeared, quickly followed by increasingly important production arrangements as its commercial interest was realised.

160

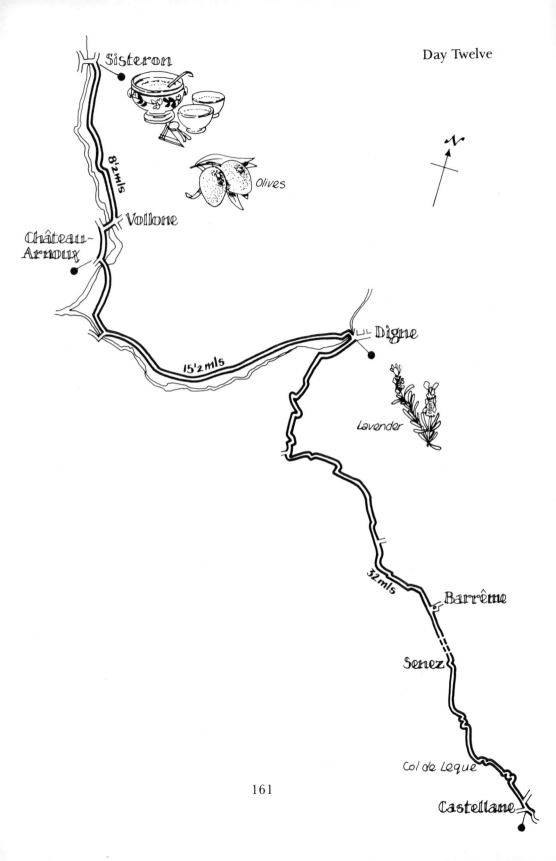

Sisteron

Olives

Vollone

Château-
Arnoux

8½mls

15½mls

Digne

Lavender

32mls

Barrême

Senez

Col de Leque

Castellane

161

In this region of Haute Provence its cultivation gradually replaced that of cereals, less well adapted to the bare soil. Then a hybrid was introduced, the lavendin, with a much higher output although with a greatly inferior perfume. The marvellous fields of purple that one sees all round Digne are covered with this lavendin.

The thermal establishment is a mile outside the town and is particularly recommended for rheumatism. Thermalism, in fact, is increasingly considered as an efficacious cure from the outset, and no longer as a last resort when all other methods have failed. Curists, when not undergoing treatment or resting, find it a splendid place for exploring the admirable surroundings.

The river Bléone passes through Digne and you follow its grandiose valley, passing close to the château of Fontenelle with its four great towers silhouetted against the hillside. At the classical eighteenth-century castle of Malijai it is recorded that Napoleon spent the night of March 4th, 1815. Its terrace dominates the city below, looking across to the Durance valley and to the mountains.

Château-Arnoux

After Malijai the horizon widens with the valley of the Durance, the road following the canal d'Oraison as far as l'Escale where there is an important dam. Then, crossing the Durance, we enter Château-Arnoux, fifteen miles from Digne. Château-Arnoux is a very pleasant little alpine resort, close to the lake of l'Escale, which is popular for boating and fishing. It is dominated by its rugged Renaissance castle, high on a rock, with elegant mullion windows. As the French say, Château-Arnoux is a *bonne-étape*, meaning a good stopping-place, and the delightful Hotel of la Bonne Étape is indeed well named, with a Michelin star to recommend its *gâteau de mostele au beurre d'orange* (mostele is a delicious Mediterranean fish), *agneau de Sisteron* and excellent pastries.

A mile further on, Volonne is another pleasant small hillside resort, with two towers remaining of its ancient defence. The road continues past olive groves, to remind us that we are still in Provence, be it on the very limit.

Sisteron

Soon after the dam of Salignac we have the first sight of the superb position of Sisteron, first and foremost a citadel. The city is situated in a curious narrow passage of the Durance, a great natural divide between Provence and the Dauphine, which has always made it a key position. Of the imposing citadel, the oldest remaining part, the keep and parapet, were built in the twelfth century, the fortifications which surround the steep rock in the sixteenth. The chapel was reconstructed in the fifteenth century. The terrace dominates the city below, looking over the valley and across to the mountains. Each year, from mid-July until the beginning of August, the *Nuits de la Citadelle* take place, a series of concerts, drama and ballet.

In the old town the high houses beside the Durance are full of charm. The church of Nôtre-Dame, formerly the cathedral, and Romano-Provençal in style, has an elegant doorway. The interior is sombre but with beautiful reredos screening the high altar and fine paintings in the side chapel. Sisteron was dear to Napoleon for it was there that he received his most whole-hearted welcome. Tomorrow you may continue along his route to Grenoble, but you will have turned your backs on Provence.

Dinner and overnight at **Tivoli**, Sisteron.

Les Santons
Place de l'Église
Moustiers-Ste.-Marie
Tel: (92) 74 66 48

A pleasant restaurant with a good, reasonably priced menu.

Closed: January and February
Credit cards: American Express, Diner's Club

HOTEL GRAND PARIS
19 Boulevard Thiers
Digne
Tel: (92) 31 11 15

A very comfortable hotel with a well-deserved Michelin star.

Tivoli
Place Tivoli
Sisteron
Tel: (92) 61 15 16

The hotel is pleasantly situated by the park and close to the Citadelle.

Closed:	15th December to 1st February
Rooms:	19
Facilities:	Restaurant, a pleasant terrace, car park
Credit cards:	American Express, Diner's Club, Visa
Food:	A varied menu
Rating:	★★

GRAND HOTEL DU COURS
Place de l'Eglise
Sisteron
Tel: (92) 61 04 51

A very comfortable hotel, unfortunately lacking a restaurant.

Closed:	15th November to 15th March
Rooms:	50
Facilities:	car parking
Credit cards:	American Express, Diner's Club, Eurocard, Visa
Food:	No restaurant but being centrally situated this presents no problem
Rating:	★★★★

SISTERON: USEFUL INFORMATION

Tourist Office:	Hôtel de Ville
	Tel: (92) 61 12 03
Population:	6572
Altitude:	482 metres
Facilities:	Railway station, hotels, camp site (La Baube)

Recipes

MENU 1 ⚜

Lunch

Tomates à la Provençal

. . .

Rougets Glacés

Dinner

Pistou

. . .

Gigot en Croute

. . .

Délice des Oranges

Wine

Rosé de Provence

Tomates à la Provençal

4 good sized tomatoes
½ cup rice
2 tbs. olive oil
flesh of half an eggplant
(aubergine)
2 cloves garlic
seasoning

Serves 4

Cut the tomatoes in halves and remove the flesh. Heat the oil, put in the rice and fry until it turns yellow but not brown. Then add the garlic and eggplant and tomato flesh, cover with water and simmer until all the water is absorbed. Season. Fill the tomatoes with this mixture, put them in an oven-proof dish, the bottom of which should have been well greased, and heat through.

Rougets Glacés (cold red mullet)

2 red mullet
½ pt. white wine

Clean the fish and put in a pan with the wine, ¼ pt. water, herbs and seasoning. Poach gently

165

sprigs of thyme and
parsley
2 onions, chopped
2 egg yolks
½ oz. cream
seasoning

Serves 4

for 10-15 minutes. Drain off the liquid and
reserve. In another pan lightly fry the onions,
add the liquid from the fish and boil fast to
reduce by half. Put on one side until cool. Stir in
the egg yolks and the cream. Place the fish on a
dish and cover with the sauce. Refrigerate. (You
may substitute other, similar varieties of fish in
this recipe.)

Pistou

4 tomatoes
6 leeks
4 potatoes
1 cup crushed basil
seasoning

Serves 4

Thoroughly wash the vegetables and chop small.
Put in a saucepan with the basil and seasoning.
Add 2 pints of water and simmer for half an
hour. Sieve and reheat.

Gigot en Croute

½ lb. uncooked short
pastry
1 leg of lamb
¼ lb. kidneys
¼ lb. mushrooms
4 oz. pâté de foie gras
sprigs of rosemary,
thyme, sage and basil
2 bay leaves

Serves 6-8

Lightly fry the chopped kidneys with the
mushrooms and add to the pâté. Stuff the leg of
lamb with this and sew up. Roast in a hot oven
for half an hour, turning once. Remove from
pan. Roll out the pastry and wrap the leg of
lamb in it, leaving the knuckle bone protruding.
Return to pan together with the herbs and
continue roasting until the pastry is golden.
Lower heat, add a small cupful of water and
continue cooking for a further 20 minutes.
Remove the herbs and use the cooking liquid for
gravy.

Délice des Oranges

1 lemon
½ pt. water
1 oz. sugar
2 tsps. cornflour

Squeeze the juice of the lemon and add ⅓ of the
water. Dissolve the sugar in the remainder of the
water and bring to the boil. Stir in the cornflour,
add the lemon juice and water and stir until it

166

2 tbs. apricot jam
2 tbs. desicated coconut
8 walnuts, chopped
4 oranges
2 oz. cream

thickens. Pour into glass bowl. Mix together the jam, coconut and chopped walnuts. Cut the oranges in halves, remove flesh, chop well and stir into the jam mixture. Add to bowl and top with cream.

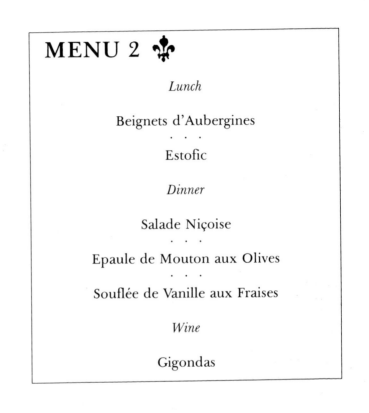

MENU 2 ⚜

Lunch

Beignets d'Aubergines

. . .

Estofic

Dinner

Salade Niçoise

. . .

Epaule de Mouton aux Olives

. . .

Souflée de Vanille aux Fraises

Wine

Gigondas

Beignets d'Aubergines

2 eggplants (aubergines)
1 egg
2 oz. flour
½ pt. milk
½ cup chopped parsley
seasoning

Serves 4

Make a batter by putting the flour and seasoning into a basin and making a well in the centre. Break egg into this and beat well. Add, gradually, the milk. Cover with a cloth and leave in a warm place for 2 hours. Wash the eggplant and slice. Leave to drain. Dip the eggplant slices in the batter mixture and fry in deep fat. Sprinkle with the parsley on serving.

Estofic

1 lb. fresh cod
4 anchovy fillets
1 oz. olive oil
3 sliced tomatoes
bouquet garni (sprigs of
thyme, parsley and a
bay leaf tied together)
¼ pt. dry white wine
½ oz. Cognac

Serves 4

Cut the cod into slices and fry for a few minutes in the olive oil. Now add the chopped anchovies, tomatoes, bouquet garni and seasoning and simmer for 20 minutes in the wine. Remove the bouquet garni, add the Cognac and serve.

Salade Niçoise

2 hard-boiled eggs
4 tomatoes, sliced
1 cup green olives
4 anchovy fillets
hearts of 2 lettuces
1 tin tunny

Serves 4

Mix all the prepared vegetables together with the tunny, anchovies, and sliced eggs and mix well with a vinaigrette (made by mixing 2 parts olive oil with one part vinegar, a pinch of mustard and seasoning). Serve immediately.

Epaule de Mouton aux Olives

1 boned shoulder of
lamb
2 oz. sausage meat
2 oz. stale bread
4 oz. green olives,
stoned and crushed
1 oz. butter
1 oz. olive oil
1 egg
seasoning

Serves 6-8

Soak the bread in milk and squeeze out. Add 2 oz. olives, the sausage meat, beaten egg and seasoning. Stuff the shoulder with this and sew up. Put in baking tin with the butter and olive oil and roast in a slow oven for 1½ hours, adding a little water if necessary. Serve surrounded with the remaining olives.

Souflée de Vanille aux Fraises

2 oz. butter
½ tsp. vanilla essence
½ pt. milk
1 oz. cornflour
3 eggs
4 oz. strawberries
2 oz. granulated sugar
1 oz. icing sugar

Serves 4

Melt the butter, stir in the cornflour and add, gradually, the milk. Stir until it thickens. Add the vanilla essence and granulated sugar. Beat in the egg yolks and, lastly, the well-whisked whites. Put into a buttered souflée dish and bake 20 minutes in a hot oven. Serve with a sauce made by well mashing the strawberries and putting in a pan with the icing sugar and ¼ pint of water. Bring to the boil and simmer 4 minutes.

MENU 3 ⚜

Lunch

Poivrons en Gelée

. . .

Sartagnade

Dinner

Tête de Veau à la Vinaigrette

. . .

Brandade

. . .

Souflée au Chocolat

Wine

Bandol (red)

Poivrons en Gelée

2 red peppers
1 cup tomato purée
1 oz. olive oil
1 oz. powdered gelatine
1 shallot

Cut peppers in halves, remove seeds and boil 5 minutes. Dissolve gelatine in a little hot water and, when on the point of setting, add to the tomato purée and well-chopped shallot. Fill

169

1 tsp. vinegar
seasoning
½ tsp. mustard powder
1 egg yolk

Serves 4

peppers with this and serve, very cold, with the mayonnaise made as follows: beat the egg yolk into a bowl with the mustard powder and beat again. Then add the oil, drop by drop, beating all the time until a creamy consistency. Add the vinegar and seasoning.

Sartagnade

1 lb. herrings, whitebait
or sprats
2 oz. olive oil
½ oz. butter
few drops lemon juice
1 tsp. vinegar
seasoning

Serves 4

Prepare the fish, removing all bones. Heat the oil and fry the fish until it sticks together, taking care that the bottom of the pan does not burn. Turn, as for a pancake, and brown the other side. Serve with a sauce made by melting the butter, then adding the lemon juice, vinegar and seasoning.

Tête de Veau à la Vinaigrette

1 calf's head
bouquet garni
2 carrots
2 onions
vinaigrette
6 capers

Serves 4-6

Soak the calf's head for 2-3 hours. Remove brains and cook these separately. Put the head in a pan with water to cover. Add the bouquet garni, the carrots and onions. Simmer about 3 hours. Serve with a vinaigrette sauce and the capers.

Brandade

1 lb. salt cod
4 large potatoes
1 oz. olive oil
¼ pt. cream
seasoning

Serves 4

Soak the cod for 24 hours, changing the water several times. Put the fish into a pan of cold water together with the peeled and sliced potatoes. Bring to the boil and simmer for 30 minutes. Drain and put in a bowl and mash well together. Add the oil, a little at a time, until the mixture is a creamy consistency. Season if necessary, add the cream and return to pan to simmer for a further 8 minutes.

Souflée au Chocolat

4 oz. plain chocolate
2 oz. soft white sugar
3 eggs
1 cup chopped walnuts
2 oz. cornflour
2 oz. butter
½ pt. milk
icing sugar

Serves 4

Break up the chocolate and put in a pan with a little water over a low heat until melted. Make a sauce by melting the butter, stirring in the cornflour and, gradually, the milk. Add the white sugar and stir until it thickens. Off the heat blend in the egg yolks and the walnuts. Fold in the melted chocolate. Lastly, whisk the egg whites and add gently. Turn into a buttered souflée dish and bake 20 minutes in a hot oven. Sprinkle with icing sugar on serving.

MENU 4 ⚜

Lunch

Céléri Remoulade

· · ·

Pissaldière

Dinner

Soupe de Poisson

· · ·

Poularde à la Provençal

· · ·

Pêche Melba

Wine

Rosé, Côte Varois

Céléri Remoulade

1 celeriac
Mayonnaise *see* Poivrons
en Gelée

Serves 4

Wash and peel the celeriac. Grate and mix well with the mayonnaise.

Pissaldière

short crust pastry
8 slices of tomato
8 onion rings
8 stoned black olives
4 anchovy fillets
8 thin slices of cheese

Serves 4

Put the pastry into a 8″ flan case and cover with, first, the tomatoes, then the onion rings in the centre of which put an olive. Criss-cross with the anchovy fillets and top with the cheese. Bake in a hot oven until golden.

Soupe de Poisson

2 lbs. mixed white fish as available
1 small tin crabmeat
bouquet garni (sprigs of parsley, thyme and a bay leaf tied together)
2 large chopped onions
seasoning
3 oz. chopped mushrooms
2 oz. olive oil
pinch of saffron

2 oz. grated cheese

Rouillé Sauce
cup stale breadcrumbs
½ red pepper
2 garlic cloves

Cut up the fish, having removed all bones, and put in a pan together with the crabmeat, bouquet garni, mushrooms, onions, olive oil, seasoning, and saffron. Add 3 pints of water, bring to the boil and simmer for 1 hour. Remove the bouquet garni and serve with the grated cheese apart and a Rouillé Sauce made as follows: chop the half pepper and fry in the oil together with the chopped garlic until tender. Soak the breadcrumbs in water, squeeze out and add, together with the olive oil and half a pint of the fish stock.

Serves 6-8

Poularde à la Provençal

1 small chicken
2 oz. margarine
2 oz. olive oil
1 stick of celery
1 small head of fennel
½ pint dry white wine
6 shallots
2 cloves garlic
8 black olives, stoned

Heat the oil and margarine, add the garlic and gently fry the chicken on both sides. Meanwhile boil the washed and well-chopped vegetables in just sufficient water to cover, until tender. Sieve, and add the chicken together with the wine and olives. Continue cooking a further 40 minutes.

Serves 4

Pêche Melba

4 ripe peaches
4 portions of vanilla
ice cream
½ pt. purée of
raspberries
sugar

Serves 4

Plunge the peaches for a few minutes into boiling water, remove carefully and plunge into ice cold water. Remove and skin. Put aside peaches in a cold place, having first sprinkled well with sugar. In a glass dish put first the ice cream, then the peaches, cut in halves, and cover with the raspberry purée.

MENU 5

Lunch

Artichauts à la Grecque

· · ·

Ratatouille aux Oeufs

Dinner

Sole Arlèsienne

· · ·

Carrés de Mouton à la Provençal

· · ·

Tarte aux Amandes

Wine

Côteaux d'Aix

Artichauts à la Grecque

8 globe artichokes
2 oz. olive oil
bouquet garni
juice of a lemon
seasoning
1 oz. coriander seeds
½ pt. dry white wine

Serves 4

With a sharp knife, cut off the leaves close to each artichoke stem. Scoop out the chokes from the centre and remove the heart. Put the hearts in a pan together with the remaining ingredients. Add a little water if necessary to cover, bring to the boil, and simmer 20 minutes. Leave to cool in the liquid.

Ratatouille aux Oeufs

8 onions
6 tomatoes
1 small vegetable
marrow
1 green pepper
1 eggplant (aubergine)
2 oz. olive oil
4 eggs
seasoning

Prepare the vegetables, removing seeds from the marrow and eggplant, and slicing them all well. Fry gently in the oil for 20 minutes, stirring to prevent sticking. Turn into an ovenproof dish and break in the eggs. Cook in a moderate oven for 10 minutes.

Serves 4

Sole Arlèsienne

4 sole fillets
1 finely chopped onion
1 tbs. chopped parsley
2 tbs. dry white wine
juice of half a lemon
2 tbs. water
2 tomatoes, peeled
seasoning

Butter an ovenproof dish and cover with the chopped onion and parsley. Lay the sole fillets on this and cover with the tomatoes, wine, water and lemon juice. Season, cover and bake 10 minutes. Add melted butter on serving.

Serves 4

Carrés de Mouton à la Provençal

1 loin of mutton
4 onions
1 clove garlic
1 green pepper, cut in
rings
4 sliced tomatoes
8 medium-sized potatoes
bouquet garni

Brown the sliced onions and garlic and add the pepper and tomatoes. Fry 2 minutes. Put the meat in an oven-proof dish and cover with the peeled and sliced potatoes, the fried vegetables, bouquet garni and seasoning. Fill up with water and simmer 1 hour.

Serves 4

Tarte aux Amandes

1 pastry flan
2 oz. slivered almonds
2 oz. soft sugar
1 oz. honey
1 oz. cream
½ oz. butter

Put the sugar, honey, cream and butter in a pan. Bring slowly to the boil and simmer 2 minutes, until creamy. Add the almonds and pour over flan. Bake 20 minutes in a moderate oven until golden.

Serves 4

Geographical Index

Index of Recipes